"Kim Rockwell-Evans has been an obsessive-con
cialist for decades. Her new book is a superbly wr
from OCD and related disorders. She is compre
technical. Her writing is entertaining and filled with expert guidance and real-
world examples. She integrates multiple evidence-based strategies, and the result
is something far more powerful and compassionate."

—**Eric Goodman, PhD**, clinical psychologist and anxiety disorder
and OCD specialist, lecturer at California Polytechnic State
University, and author of *The Mindful Freak-Out*

"Kim Rockwell-Evans has written an excellent book that is packed with information, resources, and illustrative case examples all based on the latest scientific
research. She guides you through the process of learning about OCD and engaging in proven strategies for overcoming this challenging problem."

—**Jonathan S. Abramowitz, PhD**, professor of psychology at
the University of North Carolina at Chapel Hill

"If OCD loves anything, it's a rule, and if OCD hates anything, it's breaking
those rules—so break some rules! Rockwell-Evans will walk you through busting
rules, coloring outside of the lines, and ignoring the meanest bully you have ever
had to face. This book will be an excellent resource for those in need of the
motivation to do mental martial arts and take down their OCD."

—**Patrick B. McGrath, PhD**, chief clinical officer for NOCD;
fellow of the Association of Behavioral and Cognitive Therapies
(ABCT); and member of the International OCD Foundation's
Scientific and Clinical Advisory Board (IOCDF)

"How do you loosen the grip of OCD? You pivot 180 degrees, stand shoulder-to-
shoulder with it, welcome your distress, and feel curious about what will happen
next. Sound challenging? Yes, but it's absolutely the right thing to do. Kim
Rockwell can get you there with this intriguing, no-nonsense book. You'll make
a small tweak of your belief here, try a brief experiment there—it all adds up,
and before you know it, you're skillfully taking back your life."

—**Reid Wilson, PhD**, author of *Stopping the Noise in Your Head*,
and founder of www.anxieties.com

"*Breaking the Rules of OCD* by Kim Rockwell-Evans is a helpful workbook for OCD sufferers. It lays out clearly the costs of sticking to OCD's rules, and provides many clear and workable exercises for readers to put into practice to break out of the cage those rules have created. The principles and strategies laid out in this book constitute a powerful resource, informed by scientific evidence, for those seeking to tackle their OCD."

—**Lisa W. Coyne, PhD**, CEO of the New England Center for
Anxiety and OCD, and assistant professor and senior clinical
consultant at McLean/Harvard Medical School

"Kim has written a very practical book covering many ideas and techniques to break the OCD cycle. I really appreciate the amount of exercises within the book, and the case examples help bring her ideas to life. I appreciate her unique ways of looking at OCD treatment, including developing the 'don't know' mind, and integrating principles of the Japanese martial art Aikido."

—**Stuart Ralph**, counselor and psychotherapist for children and
young people, and host of *The OCD Stories* podcast

"Long-term OCD recovery becomes quite laborious when you don't understand what reinforces and feeds repetitive, intrusive obsessions and compulsions. Kim Rockwell-Evans's book, *Breaking the Rules of OCD*, is a powerful book of strategy and insight. Kim has masterfully created a playbook that identifies the burdensome rules that keep OCD going, and provides strategic, evidence-based tools to help OCD sufferers achieve and maintain long-term OCD recovery."

—**Kimberley Quinlan**, OCD specialist, and host of *Your Anxiety
Toolkit* podcast

"Rockwell-Evans shows why many consider her an expert therapist for those with OCD. In this book, she integrates the most up-to-date and empirically supported strategies for working on your OCD. Reading this book will be like doing a course of therapy with a seasoned psychotherapist. This book is useful at any point in your treatment process."

—**Michael Twohig**, professor at Utah State University, and
coauthor of *The Anxious Perfectionist*

"This is now my go-to book to refer to clients. With a multitude of OCD books on the market, Rockwell-Evans has simplified your choice. This book is current and practical, integrating advances in OCD treatment (e.g., mindfulness, creativity, greater values, self-compassion, among others) when using exposure and response prevention (ERP) strategies. She brilliantly weaves it all together and guides you to do the same. Her wealth of knowledge and experience shines!"

—**Joan Davidson, PhD**, codirector/cofounder of the San Francisco Bay Area Center for Cognitive Therapy; assistant clinical professor in the clinical science program at the University of California, Berkeley; and author of *Daring to Challenge OCD*

"Let's face it, exposure work is hard work! When working with OCD, one-size treatment doesn't fit all. Rockwell-Evans has given us a fresh, useful, and actionable blend of evidence-based skills —combining exposure, mindfulness, acceptance and commitment therapy (ACT), and other approaches—to tackle those core psychological processes that make it hard for a person suffering with OCD to face obsessions. This is a much-needed book in the literature of evidence-based approaches for OCD. A must-read!"

—**Patricia E. Zurita Ona, PsyD**, director of the East Bay Behavior Therapy Center, and author of *Living Beyond OCD Using Acceptance and Commitment Therapy* and *Acceptance and Commitment Skills for Perfectionism and High-Achieving Behaviors*

Breaking the Rules of
OCD

Find Lasting Freedom from
the Unwanted Thoughts,
Rituals, and Compulsions
That Rule Your Life

KIM ROCKWELL-EVANS, PHD

New Harbinger Publications, Inc.

Publisher's Note

This publication is designed to provide accurate and authoritative information in regard to the subject matter covered. It is sold with the understanding that the publisher is not engaged in rendering psychological, financial, legal, or other professional services. If expert assistance or counseling is needed, the services of a competent professional should be sought.

NEW HARBINGER PUBLICATIONS is a registered trademark of New Harbinger Publications, Inc.

New Harbinger Publications is an employee-owned company.

Copyright © 2023 by Kim Rockwell-Evans
New Harbinger Publications, Inc.
5674 Shattuck Avenue
Oakland, CA 94609
www.newharbinger.com

All Rights Reserved

Cover design by Amy Daniel

Acquired by Jess O'Brien

Edited by Kristi Hein

Library of Congress Cataloging-in-Publication Data on file

FSC
www.fsc.org
MIX
Paper from
responsible sources
FSC® C011935

Printed in the United States of America

25   24   23

10   9   8   7   6   5   4   3   2   1   First Printing

Contents

Foreword

It might come as a surprise that I'm not really a fan of self-help books (but please buy all of mine). I'm probably not supposed to say that—we'll see if it makes it past the editors. But it's true. Using a self-help book can be a risky endeavor. Therapists shouldn't give clinical advice to people they've never met. No matter how many disclaimers we put in our books, we're still hoping you'll do what we recommend, but we'll never know because it's a one-way relationship. A therapist may or may not be a good fit for your needs, but you can interview them, go back and forth with them, and let them earn (or fail to earn) your trust. A self-help book can't hear you and can't ask you clarifying questions. It can only "speak" to you, and that's going to be hit or miss. In this particular self-help book, Kim Rockwell-Evans credibly sounds like a therapist who's spent a good long while getting to know you, and the odds are in your favor that if you have OCD, this book will speak to you.

Breaking the Rules of OCD lets you find yourself in the material and asks you to carefully examine how OCD affects your life. Rather than breaking down this often painful and impairing condition into subtypes, this book presents OCD as one condition with a series of mental rules. Once these OCD rules are understood, they can be broken, and once they are broken, you can be free to move about your life. The book starts with absolutely crystal-clear instructions on how to make the pages ahead work for you. Importantly, the premise of the book is that rules are adaptive.

Your compulsions are not your fault. It makes good sense why you would do what you feel you need to do to avoid the pain of OCD. It is in our nature to avoid pain. But it is also in our nature to fight, to be defiant, to reject that which constrains us. The challenge in overcoming OCD is in making it a fair fight. If we can do a functional analysis of how the OCD convinces us to stay stuck—that is, if we can see the machinery behind the OCD—we stand a much better chance.

Yes, once again you are going to be asked to consider doing something that sounds impossible. Exposure and response prevention (ERP) requires going up against OCD while resisting the very behaviors you thought were protecting you. One of the biggest challenges in mastering OCD has always been turning exposure into something you *want* to do. Why would you want to do something that makes you uncomfortable, anxious, or afraid? Rockwell-Evans uses the metaphor of aikido to explain that your opponent can be welcomed as a teacher, that taking the energy coming at you and turning it into energy that works for you is wise and effective. She also recommends acceptance and commitment therapy (ACT), mindfulness, and self-compassion tools to help you pivot and bend where curiosity and kindness make the best offense.

The book describes the many ways in which the disorder dissuades one from freedom. Rules like "you must always be certain," "all thoughts are important," and "you must always control your internal experiences" represent the arguments OCD uses to trick you into thinking you have no say in the matter. This quite brilliantly sidesteps the issue of "what about my specific obsession?" that plagues most books about OCD. She covers all of it because all of it applies to these unfair rules.

Importantly, Rockwell-Evans does more than just lay out these rules and tell how you to break them. In each chapter, she explains how the rules affect your life. *Your* life. In the book's final chapters, strategies for designing your personalized treatment plan, signs of progress to seek out, and traps to avoid are all presented masterfully. The exercises are practical and designed to apply specifically to *you* as you work through the book, not just as examples of good ideas to try in therapy.

I've never been a very good rule follower, sorry to say. Ask any of my ex-bosses. I don't like being told what to do, even by my own mind. I appreciate direction and guidelines, sure, and I'll even take advice from time to time, but *rules* make me itchy. This book may make you realize many rules you didn't even know you were following, and I hope it inspires you to stand tall and rebel.

—Jon Hershfield, MFT, Director,
　　Center for OCD and Anxiety at Sheppard Pratt

Introduction

Is obsessive-compulsive disorder (OCD) ruling your life? If so, you're not alone. And there is hope for you to break free from the paralyzing grip OCD has on you by learning to break the rules of OCD. You *can* live a fulfilling life.

Who This Book Is For

This book is written primarily for people who have been diagnosed with OCD. That said, the treatment for OCD is often counterintuitive, so it is important for loved ones to understand what it is like to have OCD and know how it is treated. This book is for them, too. Finally, busy mental health professionals may find this book helpful in understanding how to apply the treatment for their clients.

About This Book

This book is a guide to help you live a fulfilling life with OCD. The techniques outlined here integrate exposure and response prevention (ERP), acceptance and commitment therapy (ACT), and mindfulness and compassion-focused therapies—all proven effective based on clinical research.

You'll find a wealth of information, case examples, and activities to help you apply these techniques in your life—and break the OCD rules that have been interfering with your quality of life.

How to Use This Book

The book is structured for you to read cover to cover, working through each exercise as you go. Once you have worked through it in order, you may find it useful to read and practice the exercises from more challenging individual chapters again. Although this is a self-help book that you can work through by yourself, you may find it helpful to have the support of a therapist.

As you read, keep a journal and pen handy so you can work on the exercises that I guide you through. To assist with this, this book includes a number of free tools and worksheets that you can download and print at http://www.newharbinger.com/51024. Everything you need is contained in the text of the book; these online tools are supplementary, but do check them out, as the forms and prompts in particular are likely to be useful in addition to your blank journal.

You will benefit most from reading this book if you plan to follow this approach:

- Devote time each day to reading and practicing the exercises.

- Complete the suggested exercises; they're all designed to help you understand how the material applies to you.

- Practice the exercises deliberately and consistently. You have been in a behavioral pattern that keeps you stuck. The skills presented in this book are not magic; repeated practice will help you integrate them into your life. Some of the exercises are designed to be challenging. Learning new patterns of behavior is uncomfortable, so expect to venture outside of your comfort zone. I promise you, it will be worth your while.

- Approach all exercises with curiosity and an open mind. If you have tried therapy for your OCD before and found it demanding, just notice your internal responses and continue working.

- Be patient and kind with yourself. Having OCD is hard, and working on new skills to break the rules of your OCD is challenging and triggering. You may get discouraged at times while you are practicing new skills. Your success may feel up and down. This is normal; try to not let this discourage you.

- When you feel a need for support, seek it out. Support and community can offer you strength, hope, and encouragement.

- Pace yourself. If you try to work through this book too quickly, you may feel overwhelmed. Conversely, if you avoid the work and don't keep up a reading rhythm, you may be engaging in avoidant behavior. That said, it is also okay to take a break from the material if you need it.

Author's Note

I am a psychotherapist in Dallas, Texas, who specializes in treating OCD and anxiety disorders. For over twenty years, I've had the privilege of working with wonderful clients who suffer from OCD and anxiety.

When I describe particular examples of people who have OCD in this book, know that these are fictionalized composites of many people.

This book is not meant to be a replacement for consultation and psychotherapy with a mental health professional. If you have difficulty working through this book, seek out professional help. The International OCD foundation website (https://IOCDF.org) is an excellent resource to find a community that understands and can assist you in finding the right help.

CHAPTER 1

The Many Faces of OCD

Fran is standing in a puddle of water from her overflowing toilet. Again, she's used too much toilet paper in her mission to feel "clean enough." She and her ten-year-old daughter Jen are due at a family reunion in a few hours. Although Fran's family is well educated about OCD, they have expressed frustration with her history of arriving late to family gatherings or missing them altogether. So Fran is especially anxious to get there on time.

Jen, with her mother stuck in the bathroom, knows what's about to happen: Fran will ask her to gather towels and lay them on the floor to form a path to the guest bathroom. After Fran carefully walks on the towels, she will ask Jen for reassurance that she has not touched the floor with her feet.

While Fran showers for the second time, Jen will need to throw the towels in the trash bin outside and disinfect the floor. Only when all of this is done, and Fran feels clean again, can they leave. They both cry on the way to the party—and arrive when it is almost over.

If you have OCD yourself, you may recognize your own variation of the rules it imposes on your life. If you are reading this book to understand someone you know: This is what it feels like to have OCD. OCD is exhausting and a lot of work. It affects all aspects of life and hits us where it hurts the most. Many times, our attempts to deal with OCD only make it stronger, or just cause new problems. Take heart: There are treatments that work. You can live a meaningful life doing what you love while at the same time living with OCD.

Breaking free from OCD mainly comes down to understanding that much of what gives OCD power are the rigid, stifling rules it demands you follow—like the rule that *you must be absolutely certain*. Fran had a choice the day of the party: to either perform her compulsions so that she could be certain she felt clean enough or take the risk of resisting those compulsions and being uncertain. Understandably, she chose the road to certainty so she could feel comfortable at the party without worrying about feeling she was unclean, and therefore disgusting.

For the OCD sufferer, the road to certainty appears to be straightforward and offer some peace of mind. But like all attempts to get certainty, it never works.

As Fran stands in her bathroom, her feet in toilet water, her mind races:

Will I ever be clean enough? Will I accidentally contaminate my floor outside the bathroom? Did my body get contaminated by particles when I flushed the toilet? Will my day be ruined because I'm miserable obsessing about this?

It's clear that what looked like a solution—to give in to her imperative urge to make sure she's clean enough—was actually not a solution. Fran and Jen arrived late to the party, upset—and she experienced terrible anxiety about being unclean anyway. All that worry and cleaning for nothing!

Often, as you travel through the twists and turns of your compulsions, you discover that you are right back where you started—unsettled about uncertainty. Your tricky mind has put you in a position of feeling distressed and stuck. However, if you can understand how OCD works—the rules that keep you stuck in a pattern of obsession and compulsion—you can find your way out.

Understanding Obsessions and Compulsions

At the center of OCD are *obsessions*: unwanted thoughts, images, or impulses that repeatedly occur, that feel out of control, and that create a lot of distress and anxiety. When obsessions arise, a person with OCD will engage in *compulsions* in an effort to find some relief. Compulsions are urges to perform behaviors that follow a rigid set of "rules" in an attempt to avoid the outcomes you obsess over. They can be observable, external behaviors, such as checking stove burners, window locks, or doorknobs, or repeating certain actions, such as washing your hands over and over again. Or they may be more covert, mental rituals, such as praying in a certain way, or having to "undo" thoughts to erase the distressing ones.

Compulsions are upsetting and time consuming, and they often interfere with normal daily activities. You likely recognize that your obsessions and compulsions are excessive and unreasonable, but you still struggle with the need to perform these actions in order to lessen your anxiety. The alternative—*not* trying to resolve the anxiety you feel—may seem a thousand times worse.

Let's take some time to learn about the different obsessions and compulsions that can manifest, so you can begin to understand the precise contours of your own OCD.

Typical Obsessions and OCD Subtypes

While the key feature of OCD is the presence of obsessions and compulsions that are distressing enough to be disruptive to your daily activities, the particular content of obsessions and the particular compulsions that manifest can vary widely. What follows are examples of many of the common subtypes of OCD, along with the kinds of questions you might be asking yourself if you have those particular symptoms. As you read, consider whether any of the descriptions are especially resonant with your own experience.

INTRUSIVE THOUGHTS

Intrusive thoughts related to OCD involve imagining deliberate violent acts toward yourself or others. Some sufferers have violent images and urges to cause harm. Others have impulses to curse or to blurt out racial slurs.

Am I an animal killer? Michael said, *I love my dog so much. He's my baby, and I don't want anything to happen to him. Sometimes when he looks at me with such a sweet look in his eye, I get the urge to grab a knife and stab him right in the eye. I can't get rid of the terrible picture of that in my mind. I hope this isn't a sign that I'm violent. Now I have to keep my distance from him and look away.*

Am I suicidal? Cathy said, *I get a lot of dark thoughts sometimes. I've been thinking a lot about killing myself. I don't really want to, but I don't understand this urge I have to stab myself. I'm so scared I'm really going to do it, I no longer have sharp objects in my home.*

She's scared she's a killer, but I know she's not. Don said, *My wife has confessed her intrusive thoughts to me every waking moment. She will say things like: 'I just thought about throwing this glass of water in your face. I thought about stabbing someone with my keys while shopping. I thought about kicking the neighbor while I was getting the mail.' She asks me to reassure her that she isn't a killer hundreds of times a day. I'm exhausted.*

Am I like those women on the TV news who kill their children? Dorothy said, *I was so excited to find out I was pregnant. I kept thinking about how wonderful motherhood would be. I love children, and I love my baby so much. But sometimes, when I hold her, I think about snapping her neck. If I'm in the kitchen, I think about stabbing her. If I'm taking her on a walk, I think about pushing the stroller into traffic. I don't want to hurt her. If I'm psychotic and I don't know it, I should kill myself to save my baby. I will take myself out if I am a risk to my beautiful little girl.*

Am I a racist and in denial? Alberto said, As I go about my day at work, obscenities and racial slurs come into my mind when I see certain people. I really like my coworkers and my job. I don't mean these horrible thoughts that come into my mind. I worry about it later as I reflect on my day.

CONTAMINATION

Contamination-related fears are a common form of OCD. These fears can be about germs, bodily fluids, toxic material, sticky substances, or general disgust.

If I can't wash to keep clean, I am very uncomfortable. Dave said, People at work keep asking me why I wash my hands for such a long time. My washing compulsions are so exhausting. My shower in the morning takes an hour. I wash my hair two times and then tell myself I washed it. Then I go through each body part, leaving my genitals and anal opening last. I wash each body part with two pumps of soap and then state "I washed it" until I have completely washed. If I accidentally touch my body after washing my private parts, I have to start over. I don't eat or drink once I get to work because it takes too long in the bathroom. When I get home, I have to strip at the door and leave my phone, computer, and keys at my "cleaning station." I clean everything I need for the evening and run to the shower. I don't like feeling dirty.

DANGER AND HARM

These obsessions involve fears of accidentally causing harm. Examples include causing a vehicle accident, accidentally poisoning others, and careless behavior causing harm. Hit-and-run obsessions are often triggered by hitting a bump in the road or seeing something on the side of the road while driving. As a compulsion, people go back and check to see if they have hit anything. These doubts can compel a person to check the news, call the police, and search the internet to determine whether they committed a hit-and-run.

Am I responsible for a hit-and-run? Aaron said, Every time I drive, I think I've hit a pedestrian or someone's pet. All it takes is feeling a little bump in the road, *seeing something in the road or a pedestrian on the side of the road. I start thinking about whether I ran someone over, and I review every moment that I can remember. I wonder whether I'm remembering right. I often have to drive back and check. Even that doesn't stop these thoughts. I watch the news, and I check my phone for alerts from the news to see if there has been a hit-and-run. I've resorted to calling the police to see if there were any hit-and-runs. I can't get it out of my mind. Should I stop driving?*

SUPERSTITIONS

"Bad luck" words, colors, and numbers take on a magical meaning with superstitious obsessions. People hold a belief that what they associate with "bad luck" can influence future events in an unfavorable or harmful way.

The number 6 is bad luck. Dana said, *I fear something bad will happen if I do anything important on a date that relates to the number 6. The 6th, 12th, 18th, 24th, 26th, and 30th are all bad luck days where something catastrophic could happen. I also can't do anything important if the clock hits anything related to a 6. I have my way of making sure I don't order something, or contact someone, or have any other transaction related to the number 6, or something will be tainted or someone might die. It is really hard to keep this secret and avoid everything I need to so I can go on with my day. Seeing the number 6 could cause harm to someone I care about, and it would be my fault.*

SCRUPULOSITY

Religious scrupulosity obsessions are characterized by blasphemous thoughts. Fear of committing sins or offending God and doubts of salvation are followed by prayer rituals, reassurance seeking, and confession compulsions. Moral scrupulosity refers to obsessions about morality and the difference between right and wrong.

Is God mad and sending me to hell? Peter said, *I went to the most beautiful mass on Sunday morning and had an intrusive thought: Fuck Jesus. How jarring! I have sinned again because of these intrusive thoughts. To fix this, I pray to God for forgiveness, and I need to confess in a certain way. I hope God isn't mad at me and won't send me to hell. It is embarrassing to repeatedly ask the priest if I'm going to hell for thinking this. I hope I didn't really mean it and that God knows I wasn't serious about it.*

Did I cheat? Alma said, *I heard a loud noise while taking an exam and turned my head to see what was going on. Did I see someone else's test and cheat? Am I bad person? Should I tell the professor? Morality is important to me, and no matter how much I review every step of my memory, I can't figure it out.*

SEXUALITY

Sexual obsessions cover a broad range of fears about sexual acts that are taboo. This includes fear of being a pedophile or rapist, or of being sexually attracted to family members or animals.

I think it moved. Jon said, *My eighteen-month-old nephew climbed onto my lap and hit my groin. OMG. I think my penis just swelled. Maybe I'm attracted to my nephew and I'm a pedophile. Now I make excuses to not hold him for fear I really want to molest him. Whenever I see him or any other child, I double check my groin to see if I'm getting aroused.*

SEXUAL ORIENTATION

Questions about sexual orientation create uncertainty and confusion about sexual preference.

Am I gay? Betty said, *I thought my friend's blouse was so adorable on her. Maybe this means I'm gay. I have a happy marriage, and we are trying to get pregnant. My life is ruined if I'm really gay. I don't want to hurt my husband and family. Every time I see an attractive woman, I think I'm gay. Every time I have sex and don't have an orgasm, I'm sure I'm gay. I'm so confused and can't convince myself one way or the other. Does that mean I'm bi? Even though I've read every article that I can, nothing convinces me one way or the other.*

JUST RIGHT, INCOMPLETENESS, AND SYMMETRY

Obsessions in this subtype center around feelings and sensations that don't feel quite right. People who struggle with this are uncomfortable until they have the "just right" feeling. Sometimes feeling that something is incomplete may relate to not feeling right. Needing to have symmetry and exactness may drive the desire to have a "just right" feeling.

I need to feel just right. Lilly said, *It doesn't feel right if I don't sit or get up out of a chair in a certain way. It's hard to explain this feeling other than to say that I know when I don't feel right. It is embarrassing when people ask me what is wrong when I am repeatedly getting up or moving around in a chair.*

I need things to be exactly equal and even. Bella said, *I can tell if someone has moved things around. I can't leave things out of place. I have everything arranged just like I want it. Everything needs to be exactly equal and even. I don't feel right if things don't look right. Sometimes people joke with me by moving things around slightly. It is very upsetting.*

EMOTIONAL CONTAMINATION

Obsessions about being tainted by an unwanted quality of people or places are referred to as "emotional contamination." A person or place becomes associated with an unwanted characteristic that may contaminate a person struggling with this type of OCD.

Wyoming equals danger to me and my family. Ben said, *My cousin's brother-in-law who lived in Wyoming was seriously injured in an accident there. I'm afraid that anyone who has been to Wyoming will taint my family and me with tragic events. I just found out my neighbors had friends visiting them from Wyoming. It's such a chore to stay away from his family, his home, and anything associated with him. A piece of his mail was accidentally delivered to me, and I had to wash my hands thoroughly to get Wyoming off my hands. Before I knew it, two hours went by and I was still at the sink.*

RELATIONSHIPS

The hallmark of this theme is questioning oneself about a relationship. Mental "figure-it-out" rituals are performed to attempt to resolve questions such as "Is this the right relationship for me?" "Does my spouse really love me?" or "Do I love my child enough?"

Did I marry the wrong man? Jennifer said, *Maybe I'm not in love with my husband. Maybe we weren't really meant to be. I think I didn't really feel what I should have on our wedding day. He may not be the one. When I see him when he is getting dressed, I watch for signs of attraction, and sometimes his body is a turn-off. I wonder if I ever really loved him. I keep reviewing our relationship over and over again and can't get this resolved. How did I really feel on our wedding day? I've reviewed this in my mind so often I don't even know what the truth is.*

HYPERAWARENESS

This form of OCD centers around an unwanted exaggerated awareness and focus on automatic functions in the body, such as breathing, swallowing, heartbeat, and the blinking that keeps the eye surface moistened. People who struggle with this often fear they will have a loss of functioning.

Will I ever be able to socialize? Logan said, *I am aware of focusing on my swallowing and breathing throughout the day. It gets distracting, and I am self-conscious about that. I can't imagine living the rest of my life like this. I want to be able to go on dates and be with friends. I notice it even more when I'm eating or drinking. How am I going to meet people when I'm focused on swallowing and breathing? I can't imagine living my entire life overfocusing on my swallowing and breathing.*

EXISTENTIAL DREAD

Philosophical thoughts about the meaning of life and whether one's life has meaning after death can create a lot of mental rituals to try and "figure it out."

Does life mean anything? Donna said, *I find myself unmotivated to work on anything because I'm wondering whether it means anything and whether my life will be important when I'm gone. I find myself wondering what the meaning of life is. Am I doing what is right in life? I get stuck in thought loops about this, and all my reading and Google searches have left me more confused.*

Typical OCD Compulsions

Obsessions and compulsions don't necessarily correlate one-to-one with one another. Someone who has obsessions about one theme may engage in a variety of compulsions to try to avoid the discomfort of those obsessions; someone else may engage in the same compulsion yet different obsessions. OCD symptoms can be quite personal and unique to each OCD sufferer.

Here are the most common compulsions reported by those with OCD:

Decontaminating. These compulsions involve cleaning in a certain way, like getting rid of a contaminant that you think will cause harm, or washing your hands until it feels right to stop.

Checking. Checking compulsions may include making sure the stove, heater, or iron are turned off in order to avoid a disaster such as a house fire. Someone may also excessively check completed tasks to make sure they did the task correctly or didn't inadvertently write an offensive word.

Mental compulsions. These are mental behaviors carried out in a person's mind. Examples include trying to "undo" an intrusive thought with another thought, or repeatedly mentally reviewing a social event in detail to make sure you didn't blurt out an offensive remark. They can be misinterpreted as obsessions, though an obsession is a thought that *increases* your distress, while a compulsion is a thought that temporarily offers you *relief* from distress.

Repeating. Those who engage in "repeating" behavior often repeat actions because it just "feels right." Repeating behavior may also include rereading material over and over again because you worry that you haven't understood it correctly, or rewriting an email excessively because you're concerned that it's not perfect.

Counting. People who experience a counting compulsion may be trying to prevent something bad from happening, even if they don't know what the bad thing is, or to reassure themselves that they have performed a compulsion the right way. Others may find themselves overfocusing on counting objects such as ceiling tiles or steps.

Exercise: Understanding Your OCD

Now that you know a little about different forms of obsession and compulsion, here's a checklist you can use to really understand the particular thoughts and behaviors that drive your OCD. (You'll find the checklist to fill out in the free tools at http://www.newharbinger.com/51024.) Check as many items as you experience.

Obsessions

Contamination

☐ Dirt and germs

☐ Becoming ill because of a contaminant

☐ Bodily fluids (saliva, semen, urine, stool, blood, mucus)

☐ Toxic substances

☐ Spreading contaminants to others

☐ Certain unwanted characteristics of people

☐ Certain locations or places

☐ Disgust about the feeling of contamination

Violent/Aggressive

- ☐ Harming others, animals, or property
- ☐ Intrusive images or thoughts of violence
- ☐ Blurting out insults, racial slurs, or curse words
- ☐ Urge to act on an unwanted impulse
- ☐ Intrusive thoughts of self-harm

Sexual

- ☐ Sexual preference: *Am I gay? Am I straight?*
- ☐ Thoughts or images about molesting children
- ☐ Thoughts or images about having sex with animals
- ☐ Any taboo sexual thought

Hyperresponsibility

- ☐ Carelessness that results in harming someone
- ☐ Hitting a pedestrian or animal with your car in a hit-and-run
- ☐ Responsibility for a disaster such as a fire or flood

Scrupulosity

- ☐ Blasphemous thoughts
- ☐ Offending God
- ☐ Sin, fear of hell
- ☐ Doubts about salvation
- ☐ Morality—what is right and what is wrong
- ☐ Following a religious practice properly

Symmetry and Order

- ☐ Preoccupation with order and exactness

- ☐ Need for symmetry

Compulsions

Decontaminating

- ☐ Washing excessively in a certain way

- ☐ Toilet routines that are time consuming

- ☐ Cleaning objects excessively

Checking

- ☐ Excessively checking doors, faucets, appliances

- ☐ Repeatedly checking for mistakes

Order and Arranging

- ☐ Arranging things to be symmetrical

- ☐ Ordering things in a certain way

Repeating

- ☐ Tapping or touching in a certain way

- ☐ Rereading or rewriting

- ☐ Routine activities like turning light switches on and off, going in and out of a doorway

Reassurance Seeking

- ☐ Asking others for reassurance

- ☐ Online searches to find reassurance related to a fear

- ☐ Making a statement and watching how others react

- ☐ Observing someone to see if you might have upset them in some way

Mental

- ☐ Mentally undoing a disturbing thought
- ☐ Mentally reviewing events and conversations
- ☐ Counting thoughts a specific number of times
- ☐ Praying a certain way in response to an obsession
- ☐ Replacing a bad thought with a good thought
- ☐ Thinking thoughts in reverse
- ☐ Thinking thoughts, words, or phrases a special way
- ☐ Counting to special numbers
- ☐ Mental figuring out
- ☐ Making mental maps or arrangements
- ☐ Making mental lists

How did it feel to do this exercise? Keep in mind that the listed obsessions and compulsions are only the most common presentations; the list is not complete. Also keep in mind that people without OCD may at times experience mild versions of these symptoms that are not disturbing or repetitive. What ultimately determines whether you have OCD is the amount of time you spend dealing with your symptoms, and how much distress you experience when they arise.

Of course, studying a list of symptoms isn't the only way to get a sense of what your OCD looks like and how it affects your life. We can also look at the specific impacts OCD has on your life: your ability to work, study, parent, live up to your responsibilities, enjoy your leisure time and self-development, and really feel and be fulfilled.

Exercise: How Does OCD Impact Your Life?

On a separate piece of paper or in your journal, list the impact that OCD has on your:

- Relationships with family

- Social life

- Work or school

- Health

- Spiritual life

- Leisure activities

- Community

- Environment

Keep this information close. You'll use it later as you develop your plan to make choices that reduce the impact OCD has on these important areas of your life.

How You Can Break Free of OCD

You may have found it daunting to read about all OCD's different manifestations and to explore your OCD in the previous activities. Even with good therapy, most people with OCD find that its impact tends to wax and wane throughout life. But that doesn't mean there's nothing you can do about it. If you can learn to experience what triggers your anxiety and practice more flexible responses when anxiety arises, you can learn to relate to your anxiety differently, so it doesn't control what you do and rule your life.

This may sound incredible now. But the therapy that informs the treatment program in this book—cognitive behavioral therapy (CBT)—can help you do this.

CBT applies to a variety of behavioral therapies that help you examine the interactions between your thoughts, behaviors, feelings, and bodily sensations. Using this approach, you'll come to understand the cycle of thoughts and behaviors that maintains your OCD—from initial obsession, to compulsion, to temporary relief, to recurring anxiety.

At the heart of your therapy is a form of CBT called *exposure and response prevention* (ERP). ERP is all about gradually exposing yourself, in a measured, step-by-step way, to situations that provoke your anxieties and obsessions. By purposely exposing yourself in a safe environment, you can make contact with the thoughts and feelings you might be avoiding, and practice and learn different ways of responding to the things that trigger your OCD.

We'll also use a few other therapies in our approach in this book. One I've already mentioned is acceptance and commitment therapy (ACT). This behavioral and exposure-based therapy emphasizes developing psychological flexibility—that is, the ability to stay in contact with how you feel even when it's painful, so you can flexibly and realistically decide what you want to do, rather than acting based on habit. With ACT, you learn to be more aware and accepting of your discomfort, rather than blindly reacting to it, while you do what matters to you. So one goal of ACT is to live a valued life even when you're experiencing anxiety, rather than letting that anxiety and your OCD determine what you will or won't do.

Three core pillars to ACT—awareness, openness, and engagement—are relevant to the work we'll do in this book.

The first pillar, awareness, is about developing present-moment awareness and a flexible sense of yourself that isn't defined by your thoughts, feelings, and sensations. The second pillar, openness, involves the practice of willingness—being open and willing to experience whatever you're experiencing, especially when it's difficult. The reality is, OCD sucks. It's no wonder that often, when we're stressed and in pain, or fearing that something terrible might happen if we expose ourselves to this situation or don't do that compulsion, our first instinct is to react—to avoid the triggering situation, do the compulsion, check, seek reassurance, decontaminate. But as loudly as OCD might scream at us to do this, we *do* actually have a choice. It starts with being willing to let the anxiety and the fear we feel be there, without rushing to react to it by avoiding or attempting to control our internal experience—both of which feel good or productive in the moment but are ultimately doomed to fail.

The mindfulness practices you'll be learning in this book (see chapter 4) will help you increase your capacity to practice skills associated with the awareness and openness pillars.

The third pillar, engagement, is about identifying the personal values that can guide you to behaviors that are consistent with your values, rather than dominated by obsessions, compulsions, and fears.

There's an important thread that runs through all of this: self-compassion. People with OCD have a tremendous amount of shame, guilt, and self-criticism, all of which create more suffering, making you feel hopeless and worthless. If you can cultivate self-compassion—the ability to see yourself as a suffering person who's doing the best they can, deserving kindness and understanding even as they work to change dysfunctional patterns—this can help motivate you to take actions that will help you change, much more than punishing yourself will.

The work you'll do in this book won't always be easy. To live well with OCD, to break free of the rules it imposes on your life, you'll need to integrate various insights and practices from ERP, ACT, and self-compassion into your daily life, and to persist with them. This may feel daunting at first. To help temper that feeling, this book will give you a roadmap and a variety of skills you can implement. And as you work through the exercises and practice the skills, you'll discover it's possible to confront and overcome the anxiety that currently rules your life. And you'll be able to ensure that it's *you* taking charge of your life—not your OCD.

In the next chapter, we'll look at the cycle of experience that maintains OCD—the loop from obsession, to compulsion, to temporary relief, and back to even stronger obsessions—and the specific rules about what *should* and *should not* happen that keep you stuck in this cycle. It's the first step to using ERP to break free.

CHAPTER 2

The Maintenance Cycle of OCD

As you learned in the last chapter, OCD is fueled by a particular stance toward your own experience—specifically, an instinct to avoid situations that trigger the discomfort of obsessive thoughts, or to control what you feel, when obsessions arise, and stop yourself from feeling that way. But fear and anxiety, as uncomfortable as they are, are parts of the normal human experience—even when you're dealing with extreme forms of them, as with OCD. And you can't really fight them off. Avoiding them only leads to more pain, not less.

However, if you can understand the nature of fear, and the particular ways your OCD brain latches onto fear and uncertainty and devises rules you must follow in a mistaken bid to stay safe from the threats it perceives, you can begin understanding your OCD from a functional perspective. That is, you can see specifically what triggers your compulsive behavior, and how your responses to a trigger—the thoughts, feelings, and bodily sensations that follow—trap you in a cycle of obsession and compulsion. You can also come to understand your true values—the things you really want your life to be about—which can help guide you to confront and change the OCD cycle, using ERP.

Let's begin by looking at how fears can get us stuck in avoidant and compulsive behaviors.

How We Acquire Fear

Behind the scenes in our mind, we are always creating associations between objects, people, locations, smells, sounds, and sights—figuring out what they mean for us, and fashioning rules that go on to guide our behavior around them in the future. The human brain is powerful; it can relate anything to anything. This evolved for safety and survival, helping our ancestors learn by association where the best food and water could be found, or where dangerous predators might live.

Your brain is also a great storyteller and can justify how you relate anything to anything else. As you relate one thing to something else, more relationships are created, forming a network of associations. And ultimately, even nonsensical associations can be convincing to your mind, especially if your mind believes that those associations will keep you safe.

To illustrate this, let's look at Lilly's experience walking her dog, Rolph.

For Lilly, her walks with Rolph are a special time, because she loves him and finds walking a refreshing way to start the day—and Rolph gets so excited to go on a walk! One day, while walking, Rolph and Lilly passed a discarded surgical mask lying on the ground. Lilly notices the mask and starts to feel a queasy sensation in her stomach as she thinks What if there's COVID on that mask? As they walk on, she tries to remember whether Rolph touched the mask. She isn't sure whether she touched it with her shoe either. They immediately return home, where Lilly leaves her shoes outside and doesn't allow Rolph inside the house. She has her roommate take Rolph to the veterinarian and throws her shoes in the trash, just in case. Every time she thinks about taking Rolph on a walk, even touching Rolph, or her morning walks, she fears catching COVID. Lilly has now acquired an intense fear. In this example, her brain has associated her experience walking her dog with the danger of catching a serious illness.

As time passes, Lilly continues keeping her distance from Rolph, no longer petting or walking him. She begins avoiding all dogs, and she stops allowing any shoes indoors.

Lilly has learned that:

Walking on the street = danger

Rolph = danger

Lilly's shoes = danger

Lilly's fear has generalized to include all dogs, shoes, and walking outside. Once someone with OCD makes an association between fear and something innocuous, it may generalize to include situations with similar cues—such as Lilly now feeling anxious whenever she sees any dog at all being walked outside.

This is the brain making sure we're "better safe than sorry." These types of generalizations were adaptive for our ancestors living in hunter-gatherer societies, and they can be protective of us—if we are confronted with a *real* threat. For Lilly, generalization made her afraid of things that aren't *necessarily* threats—like her dog, or other dogs, or walks, or the outside world. They shut her away from things she cared about and made her life seem small.

Ultimately, we become compelled to follow the rigid rules of OCD by the particular associations we make, and the way these associations lead us to acquire fear of particular things or situations that may not actually be merited by the things or situations themselves.

The Rules of OCD

We all live according to many personal, cultural, and governmental rules. Those rules can be adaptive and important for learning effective ways to respond to the world around us. Rules such as "Look both directions before crossing the street," "Don't touch a hot stove," and "Don't approach a coiled rattlesnake" are examples of rules that can help us survive.

Rules also help us organize actions and behaviors toward specific ends. After all, what would a sports game be without rules? How would we solve mathematical equations without rules?

Note, however, that all these rules are adaptive in their contexts. A given rule is useful only if it truly applies to the situation it's being used to navigate. For instance, if you refuse to water the flowers because the hose is coiled up like a snake, that wouldn't be adaptive. A coiled-up object isn't always dangerous.

Rules can also be inflexible and rigid. OCD can operate in such a way that you develop rigid rules you must follow to alleviate your fear that something bad will happen. A person without OCD may check the stove burners and water faucets one time before they leave on a trip, because that's a rule they have established for the sake of basic responsibility as a tenant or homeowner. But for someone with OCD, the anxiety they feel—*Did I turn off the stove? Did I turn the faucets all the way off? What if the house burns down or floods?*—may be persistent. They may need to check the faucets and burners multiple times; they return home after they've driven a few blocks to check again; they may call their neighbor from their vacation rental to ask them to check again. In this case, the rule (*Check all the faucets and burners when you leave the house to make sure they're off*) becomes stifling and can make their life feel limited and very stressful.

Does this happen to you? If so, you might find that following the rules quickly leads you into a double bind. If you don't do what the obsession tells you—refusing to check the faucets before you go—you fear something bad will happen. If you do it—obsessively check the faucets multiple times before you go—your life is still limited and full of worry. After all, it's stressful to do something over and over again, and even if you do all your checking before you leave, the chance of nothing bad happening after that is never 100 percent.

Also, when your behavioral response is to blindly follow the rules OCD has made for you, you may miss information in your internal or external environment that may contradict the rule you are following. Ultimately, every time you succumb to your obsession and perform an action demanded by your anxiety and fear, you are strengthening the brain connection between the rule and a feeling of relief you get by following the rule. As you continue to follow these rules, their power is reinforced and strengthened until you're in a maintenance cycle that can make you feel like your mind is stuck in a loop. As this cycle continues, and you consistently follow these rules, you become less likely to flexibly respond to your anxiety. And you move away from things that matter to you.

What follows is a brief description of the rules that OCD forces you to follow, which keep you stuck in the loop of obsessions and compulsions.

- You must always control your internal experiences. If you do not control all the thoughts, feelings, images, and sensations in your body, you will continue to suffer.

- You must be certain. You need to have 100-percent certainty in order to be safe.

- You must pay attention to every single thought you have. Your thoughts are important and may have power to cause or prevent harm.

- You must be concerned by the presence of any anxiety, as it signals that you are in danger. Your experience with anxiety must mean that something bad is imminent.

- You alone are responsible if you fail to prevent harm. You have the power to prevent something terrible from happening.

- Everything must be "just right." If things are not in perfect order, or you don't feel "just right," you will suffer.

- You must always keep your OCD hidden from others. You are broken. No one who finds out about it will understand you.

As you'll discover in this book, none of these rules are really true. But—as with the associations Lilly made after her walk with Rolph, earlier in the chapter—they *feel* true. And as you follow them, you perform compulsions as strategies to avoid the fear and anxiety that they create. These rules fuel the anxious thoughts that turn into the narratives about harm—and your responsibility for dealing with it—that keep you spiraling in a mental loop in your mind.

Let's look at some of the psychological and behavioral processes that give the rules of OCD power in your life: biased information processing, attempts to control your thoughts, and behaving in ways intended to reduce the anxiety you feel.

How OCD Maintains Its Power

Again, our brains can get confused and activate our threat system unnecessarily. If your mind perceives a threat where there isn't actually a threat, you will experience fear that you may interpret as danger. (Imagine reacting to a life-sized, cardboard Smokey the Bear as if it were a real bear charging at you.) What's more, the more you focus on what you think is a threat, the less you can be aware of other information in your environment and your reactions to it. And as you disregard information in your overall environment, your mind's narrow focus contributes to more misconceptions.

Let's look at a few examples:

- A person with contamination obsessions may see something on the ground that looks like blood, which they associate with HIV. So they hyperfocus on other things in their environment that look like blood, because they're so afraid of getting HIV—even though not only is most of what they focus on not blood, but it's impossible to get HIV from the mere sight of blood.

- A person with hit-and-run obsessions may drive back to a spot where they thought *Maybe I hit someone* to check for signs of an accident, even though they've already checked, there's no blood on their car, and it's a busy intersection where people would have stared and shouted if there actually had been an accident.

- If someone has an overwhelming fear of cursing or saying a racial slur, this fear may produce responses like anxiety, obsessively checking emails and documents for words that may be offensive, and needing to attend to words that begin with certain letters.

Another type of misconception occurs when people selectively remember fear and distressing experiences related to obsessions and ignore anything that challenges their assumptions. For example, imagine that one day, while playing with your neighbor's dog, it vomits on you. Even though you have enjoyed playing with the dog hundreds of times before, you now selectively remember how gross and contaminated you felt, more than the many pleasant times you've had with the dog, so you go out of your way to avoid the dog.

When you encounter a situation you interpret in such a biased way, you may have a strong physiological response to a perceived threat—such as rising heart rate, sweating, and a sick feeling in your stomach—that then creates even more anxiety. In response, your mind might interpret these physiological responses as a confirmation that your anxieties are true—and put even more pressure on you to avoid the anxiety-causing situations you fear.

Or you might come into contact with those situations and feel fear and anxiety that seem intolerable, and you might try to suppress your fearful, anxious thoughts, rather than succumbing to compulsions. But trying to suppress unwanted thoughts actually does the opposite—it makes them harder to get over and more likely to recur. So trying to suppress these thoughts only makes you feel out of control.

All your attempts to reduce anxiety—whether through compulsions, suppressing anxious thoughts, or avoiding the situations that make you anxious—prevent you from having the experience of learning what would actually happen if you allowed yourself to face your fears. And as you continue using these strategies, you lose confidence in your ability to cope with life. This can be exhausting and demoralizing.

How can you begin to interrupt this cycle and free yourself from OCD's rules and the fears it forces you to make so central in your life? The first step is to discover the relationship between your obsessions, compulsions, and avoidance behavior.

Your Maintenance Cycle of OCD

In this section, we will examine what happens before, during, and after your compulsive or avoidance behavior, so we can see exactly what triggers it—which situations or stimuli you encounter in the world that activate your fear. Then we'll look at the details of your immediate response, such as thoughts, feelings, and bodily sensations. Finally, we'll explore the effects your compulsive behavior has on you in the short and long term.

Exercise: Understanding Your Maintenance Cycle of OCD

This exercise guides you through making a functional analysis of your OCD by charting how your OCD manifests through the following sequence of steps.

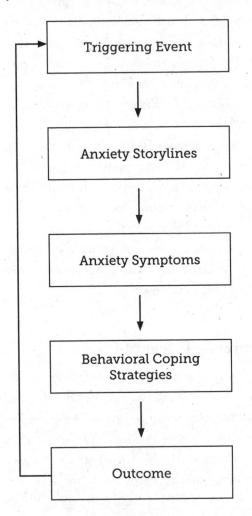

You can download the Maintenance Cycle of OCD form (available at http://www.newharbinger.com/51024) or just follow the steps as you read each section, taking notes in your journal. We'll use your responses to create your ERP plan in chapter 3.

Step 1: Triggering Event

What triggers your OCD? Often, the OCD cycle begins with an event that left you with an uncomfortable association between the event and something innocuous, like a dog or a particular color, and it can be triggered by encounters with that same stimulus in the present. Identify the location and who or what triggered your OCD response. All of these details make up the context of your OCD symptoms. In addition to external events, triggers can also include internal sensations, thoughts, images, and urges. Write your triggering events in the Triggering Event box.

For example, Lilly's triggering event is finding a face mask on the ground that she fears she or Rolph might have touched while walking in their neighborhood.

Step 2: Anxiety Storylines

What stories are you telling yourself in response to your triggering event? These thoughts tend to turn into narratives that keep you stuck in the cycle of anxiety and OCD behavior. Write them in the Anxiety Storylines box.

For example, the storylines that Lilly experiences center around the danger of contamination with COVID, and the fear that she or Rolph may get infected with COVID and die.

Step 3: Anxiety Symptoms

Where do you feel your anxiety in your body? How do you know you are anxious? Does your heart beat faster, does your stomach churn, do you sweat? Begin noticing what sensations you feel in your body when you are afraid. Write them in the Anxiety Symptoms box.

For example, Lilly feels queasy in her stomach, tightness in her chest, and a little short of breath.

Step 4: Behavioral Coping Strategies

Identify your compulsions, avoidance behaviors, and behaviors that make you feel safe. What strategies do you use to avoid what you fear may happen? What compulsions do you engage in? What do you do to feel safer? The strategies can be both behaviors that are observable by others and unseen mental behaviors. Write these in the Behavioral Coping Strategies box.

For example, since her scare, Lilly avoids Rolph, walking, shoes, all dogs, and being outdoors. Her compulsions include reassurance seeking and continually mentally reviewing her walk on that day when she and Rolph saw the mask on the ground. She repeatedly checks her temperature and oxygen level for signs of COVID.

When your fear response is triggered by a situation in which actual danger is unlikely, your response will involve actions that are at least a little bit helpful short term—you might feel a brief respite from your anxiety, or at least some sense that you've "done something"—but not helpful long term. The feelings of relief don't last, and the anxiety and obsessive thoughts inevitably return, often stronger than before.

Step 5: Outcome

What happens after you avoid what you are afraid of or perform compulsions?

Do you feel relief from your anxiety? How long does this relief last? What are some other emotions that you feel? How long do those feelings usually last? Do you notice a change in your physiological response? Write these in the Outcome box.

For example, Lilly's short-term outcome was feeling relieved after she avoided her triggers or performed compulsions to make her anxiety go away.

Now, think about the long term. What are some problems your compulsive and avoidance behavior cause you in your life? Now think about how you would like your life to look. Think about your personal goals for accomplishments, relationships, career, and self-care. Does your behavioral response to your obsessions move you toward what is important to you? Do you find that your behavior is more inflexible? Does your confidence in your ability to face your fears diminish further? Add these details to the Outcome box.

For Lilly, her life became limited by her anxiety about dogs, walking, shoes, even the whole outdoors. She missed taking Rolph on their relaxing walks. Over time, Lilly noticed that the relief she felt was short-lived. Eventually the relief was so minimal that her compulsions and avoidance behavior worsened and impacted her quality of life.

When you've completed your Maintenance Cycle of OCD form, think about what the experience was like for you. You probably see that you've avoided what makes you uncomfortable and performed compulsions because this gives you temporary relief from that discomfort. That's totally understandable: Who wouldn't seek relief from anxiety? It's universal among humans to avoid feeling pain. And when our behavior is reinforced in a desirable way—with our pain lessening, even if it's just in the short term—we're going to repeat the behavior that gave us that relief. So your behaviors make sense. But when your behaviors are driven by OCD, the trouble is that as you continue to experience temporary relief when you perform your OCD behaviors, you are actually strengthening the hold that OCD has on you.

You may feel so beat up by your OCD that you don't believe you are strong enough to stop using compulsions and avoiding what triggers your anxiety. This book is going to teach you proven skills to lessen your dependence on these behaviors. As you practice these skills, you can learn that you can experience—and tolerate—discomfort in the short term to gain long-term relief.

It can be hard work to allow yourself to feel the short-term discomfort, but you can do it. Many people have used these techniques successfully. You have agency to make the changes to your behavior that will loosen OCD's grip on you.

Let's explore this idea of agency with a quick exercise.

Exercise: Exercising Your Agency

1. (Complete this step before reading the next step.) In a seated or standing position, tell yourself, either out loud or silently in your mind, to raise your right arm, put it down, then raise your left arm, and put it down. Repeat this sequence several times until it becomes automatic.

2. Repeat step 1, but this time don't follow the directions exactly. For example, maybe when you tell yourself to raise your right arm, you raise your left foot instead. Do random variations on the directions several times.

What did you notice about the difference between following or not following the directions you gave yourself? For example, did you feel different sensations in your body? Did it take a moment to consciously not follow the directions?

Your mind can give you some strong directives that you automatically follow. Sometimes following these directives is useful to you; other times they make your life inflexible. The more flexible you are in responding to your OCD, the more likely it is that you can make decisions that lead you toward a life you dream of.

It's not your fault that you have OCD. It's natural to resist what is uncomfortable, and your brain just happens to seek relief from discomfort through compulsive and avoidance behaviors. What's more, you don't have a choice about what you feel inside. Your brain automatically creates thoughts, images, feelings, and bodily sensations because that's what it is designed to do. But you can learn how to break the rules of OCD in a way that works for you. By taking it one step at a time as you work through this book, you can break down the steps to recovery into small bits by changing your responses to your OCD behaviors.

One step to reclaiming your agency is by personifying the voice of your OCD; that is, by giving it an identity. There are a variety of ways to do this. You may simply want to identify your obsessions and refer to them as your "OCD thoughts." Or you may want to create an image of your OCD in your mind. Your OCD can be loud, strong, and convincing, like a roaring monster, or have powerful jaws with sharp teeth. Conceptualizing it in this way can help you step back and observe your mind rather than be entangled with the messages it sends. By doing this, you can begin making decisions that are healthy for you. Instead of allowing your OCD to control your behavioral response to fear, you have disentangled your wise brain from the part of your brain that tells you those anxious stories that have you performing those behaviors. You'll learn to change your relationship with your OCD thoughts, images, and the sensations it creates in your body.

You can choose your life over the rules of OCD. Granted, change is hard for everyone. For you to experience flexible living that allows you to make choices independent from what OCD dictates, you must venture out of your comfort zone. But I think you'll find that engaging in meaningful activities with people you love can make the feared consequence of not following the rules of OCD less important.

To begin figuring out which activities will be truly meaningful for you, let's consider what your values are.

Clarifying Your Values

Your values guide you in a freely chosen direction that creates meaning in your life. For instance, your values might be *creativity, achievement, being a good parent, contributing to the community*, and so on. Choosing actions that are based on your values and lead you to the life you want is much more important than trying to eliminate your fear and anxiety by following the rules of OCD, even though the OCD is telling you the opposite. And clarifying your specific values can create a guide for you to follow as you choose a direction for your life, beyond simply repeating the exhausting, demoralizing cycle of OCD. When you make choices that move you in a direction that matters, you change your focus to what is meaningful rather than what will give you temporary relief from your anxiety.

What would you say your values are? Perhaps you can think right away of values you hold—of aspirations that can structure your behavior and make your life meaningful. Or maybe your mind's just gone blank. It can be hard to identify what your values are, especially if you've been struggling with OCD for a while. Often, our values are connected to the things we avoid no less than the things we love and appreciate. If you find it especially challenging to identify what matters to you, try looking at what causes you emotional pain—especially as it relates to your OCD, which tends to hit you where you hurt the most.

Recall Lilly and her dog Rolph. Lilly experienced sadness and anxiety after she stopped taking care of Rolph. When she explored her values, she realized that one of those values was being a good dog owner. She treasured her love for Rolph and the companionship they shared—and her anxiety and discomfort were causing her to neglect Rolph. She realized she could also reconnect with this important value of taking care of her beloved companion, and that doing so would require that she stay in contact with her painful emotions as she develops a plan to stop avoiding Rolph and to start taking walks again. She has the choice to become more comfortable with feeling some anxiety, which will then allow her to go out with Rolph. If she does, she will have companionship with Rolph and all the good feelings that come with it to balance out the fear that might arise as she learns skills to confront her obsessions and anxieties.

Exercise: Finding Values from Pain

Grab a blank sheet of paper, or turn to a new page in a notebook, and take a moment to identify areas where OCD has contributed to emotional pain in your life. Write down situations where your OCD has caused you to act against your values.

Now turn your paper over and write down your values for the same areas. For example, you might have the value of being a consistent, loving, and supportive partner in a relationship, but your OCD might cause stress that makes it harder for you to be the kind of person you want to be in your partnership.

Discomfort Is Normal and Okay

When you explore your values, it can be a messy process for everyone because connecting with what is meaningful creates a full range of emotions. As you try to make decisions based on your values, your thoughts, feelings, and bodily sensations can create barriers.

It is crucial, when exploring your values, that you be nonjudgmental toward yourself. Because this exploration will show you ways in which you may not be living consistent with your values, you may experience guilt and shame. Remember that nobody lives 100-percent consistently with their values. We all struggle sometimes to do the right thing every single time, especially in those moments that it's just easier to let our values slide than to stick to them. Your compulsions or avoidance behavior in response to some frightening obsessions may make it difficult to live in a way that's consistent with some of your values. But by being conscious of this and exploring it, you can better understand ways you can shift your behavior to be the person you want to be. In short, knowing your values helps guide you to exercise agency over your behavior to make the changes that you want in your life.

OCD Can Hijack Your Values

OCD can hijack your values by making you think that your compulsions are serving your values, when often they are undermining them. For example, you could spend a lot of time performing checking compulsions before bedtime to be sure you locked the door and turned off appliances to protect your family. These time-consuming rituals actually rob you of sleep and interfere with your participating in daily family activities; the compulsions are actually taking you away from your family rather than allowing you to be there for them.

The following exercise will help you explore your own values as a step toward understanding what is most important to you.

Exercise: Values Exploration

You'll use the following questions as writing prompts—but before you start writing, take a moment to slow down. Allow twenty minutes to one hour for this exercise.

1. Find a comfortable seat in a quiet place where you won't be disturbed.

2. Close your eyes and focus on your breathing for about thirty seconds. Allow your mind to reflect on what matters to you.

3. Now, for each question, write from your heart for twenty minutes. You can either answer the prompts one after the other or do one prompt per day.

   - What would you like your life to stand for?

   - What kind of person do you want to be?

   - What is important to you?

Some life domains you may want to include are family, friends, intimate relationships, career, education, leisure, spirituality, health, community, and the environment.

Values-Driven Living Is a Practice

Living a values-driven life requires you to be present and make intentional choices in the service of something important to you. This is a dynamic and flexible process that is lifelong. To live a values-driven life, ask yourself the following question as you start your day: *What can I do today to move in a direction that matters?*

When you are moving in a direction that's important to you, the path before you broadens. When you are moving away from your values, then your choices are narrow and inflexible—that's how OCD works. For example, if you have a value of being an innovative and productive employee, and you're distracted by worrying because your meeting is starting at a time that you consider bad luck, you won't be focused on the meeting and on contributing your ideas. Periodically during your day, ask yourself *Is my behavior taking me toward the life I want, or is it taking me away from what I value?*

At the end of the day, reflect on your day by asking yourself *What did I do today that was in the service of one of my values?* and *What did I do today that was not in service of my values?* When you track this daily, it helps you shift your focus from your OCD symptoms to doing what is meaningful to you.

Points to Remember

Anxiety is part of the human experience; it can be adaptive, keeping us safe, or it can get in the way of how we need to function. When you experience obsessions, your brain misinterprets certain situations, objects, and experiences so they cause anxiety, which then causes avoidance and compulsive behaviors—in a nutshell, OCD. OCD operates based on rules that restrict your life choices. The more you follow these rules, continuing to respond to your obsessions with compulsions and avoidance behaviors, the stronger OCD's grip on you will be. Now you're taking steps to break those rules and free yourself from that grip.

You have worked hard in this chapter to identify the values you want to live by. You've also done a functional analysis to uncover how your OCD operates in your life as a barrier to living those values. With these findings captured on paper, in the next chapter you will use them to develop and put into action an ERP plan, designed to help you exercise agency over your behavior and take manageable steps to face your fears. As you work through this book, you will continue using your findings to inform your ERP planning.

CHAPTER 3

Breaking Free with ERP

With your current OCD maintenance cycle mapped out, you can use it to begin planning the exposure practices that will help you overcome your compulsions. In this chapter, you will learn to set up values-based goals and take steps to plan and implement your ERP strategy to achieve those goals. First, let's take a look at what ERP is and how it works.

Exposure and Response Prevention

ERP is a practice of confronting the disturbing thoughts, images, feelings, and situations that trigger your anxiety. Decades of clinical research consistently demonstrates the effectiveness of ERP in reducing the symptoms of OCD. By using ERP, you can weaken the association between what triggers your anxiety and the compulsions or avoidant behaviors that you respond with. When you stop performing behaviors that keep you stuck in your OCD cycle, your relationship with your anxiety will change. You may find that your internal experience with anxiety is more tolerable than you've imagined it could be. You may find it rewarding to engage in valued activities that you'd been avoiding because of your OCD. And as you learn how to function better even when anxiety is present, you may begin to feel more confident.

ERP has two components. *Exposure*, the E part, involves contact with the stimuli that trigger your OCD. *Response prevention*—the RP part—is what you do to prevent yourself from performing compulsions. For example, if Lilly tries to confront her fears of contagion by using the exposure component of ERP—taking Rolph on a walk near the area where they saw the discarded mask—but she returns home and still asks her roommate to wash Rolph's feet while she searches online for information on how long COVID remains contagious on the sidewalk, she has not prevented the compulsive response; she's simply changed it. For Lilly to use ERP successfully, she needs to stop herself from performing those compulsions after she initiates the exposure—no asking for reassurance, searching online, asking others to help her decontaminate, or any other effort to respond to her obsession.

You'll be learning how to create exposures that trigger your compulsions, then developing a plan to prevent these behaviors. Using values that you identified in the past chapters, you will learn how to focus on your priorities—what you'd like to be able to do—and use those values to direct your behavior. Then you will purposely put yourself in situations where you experience what triggers your OCD. You'll purposely choose to not engage in avoidant behaviors or compulsions when faced with your fears, keeping your values in mind as a motivator. With practice, you'll learn that you can allow uncomfortable thoughts, images, feelings, and sensations without being hooked into compulsive behaviors to try to make it go away.

As you design your exposure plan, you will also develop a response prevention plan for each ERP task you undertake that will guide you in how to not engage in compulsions or avoidant behavior after completion of your exposures. Again, it's crucial to have an RP plan for each exposure you plan to practice. Without this, you are unlikely to learn from your exposure practice.

How ERP Works

Let's look at three important views on how ERP can create effective change, helping you learn that you can face your fears and live according to your values even when you are afraid.

Emotional processing theory (Foa and Kozak 1986) tells us that the mind leads us to avoid behavior we perceive as dangerous. ERP can modify this fear structure so you can learn how to consciously choose behaviors that align with your values rather than behavior that supports your fear response. With repeated practice, you can disconfirm the beliefs that activate your OCD cycle. This model suggests that when your brain gets used to experiencing what triggers your anxiety, your anxiety will diminish. This process is called *habituation*.

Another view of how change occurs during exposure is described in the inhibitory learning model (ILM) (Craske et al. 2008). When your brain creates fear associations—such as Lilly associating Rolph with danger, because it was while she was walking him that she encountered the cloth mask on the ground—they can't be erased. The good news is that with ERP, you can experience the triggers that your brain has associated with fear and create new brain pathways that allow you to tolerate your anxiety *without* needing to perform compulsive behaviors to avoid it. When you learn a larger repertoire of responses to fear, your brain will be more likely to respond to a new association. Your brain now has new learning that *inhibits* the original fear learning.

Acceptance and commitment therapy (ACT) (Hayes, Strosahl, and Wilson 2012) emphasizes learning to face your fears by developing a more flexible way of responding to them so you can do what is meaningful to you even when you feel scared. ACT is about focusing on values even while feeling the discomfort of obsessions and urges, rather than trying to reduce the level of anxiety. What's important from an ACT perspective is that you respond to what is uncomfortable with flexibility. As you learn to choose experiences consistent with your values, the paralyzing effect of your OCD gets weaker. You learn that you can do what matters and experience anxiety at the same time. Anxiety and fear are no longer barriers to living a life of value.

All three approaches have this in common: when you repeatedly confront your fears, you can loosen the grip that your OCD has on you. When you respond to your obsessions differently, you are creating new experiences with what triggers you that are inconsistent with the frightening stories that your mind has created.

Now that you have an idea of the core mechanisms of change that make ERP effective, let's look at how to actually use it in your life.

Creating an ERP Menu

To create your menu, you'll compile a personalized list of OCD behaviors that keep you stuck in your OCD cycle, with the goal of learning how to confront them. You'll break them down into small manageable tasks, which will help you learn to accept uncomfortable feelings in the service of your values.

For each situation on your menu, you will rate your distress level on a scale of 0 through 10, with 0 being no distress at all and 10 being the highest level of distress. You can refer to your ERP menu as you choose which exposures to practice.

Here's Lilly's ERP menu and her ratings:

Touch shoes: 4

Wear shoes without washing the soles: 5

Pet Rolph without verifying that he hasn't been outside: 5

Touch Rolph's leash: 6

Walk to the mailbox and get the mail: 6

Sit outside on the back porch holding Rolph: 6

Allow Rolph to pee and poop in the backyard: 7

Play with Rolph in the backyard: 7

Sit outside on the front porch holding Rolph: 7

Attach Rolph's leash and walk around the backyard: 7

Walk with Rolph in the front yard: 8

Walk with Rolph to the mailbox: 8

Walk around the block with Rolph: 8

Walk with Rolph in the neighborhood away from the street where we saw the mask: 9

Walk with Rolph on the street where the mask was: 10

Lilly's ERP menu includes activities related to walking and enjoying Rolph. Notice that touching her shoes would be challenging but manageable, whereas walking Rolph in the neighborhood would be highly anxiety provoking and challenging for her. The information from her ERP menu will help Lilly design her plan for each exposure task as she begins to work on it.

Now it's time for you to build your own menu.

Exercise: Creating an ERP Menu

An ERP menu is simply a list of situations you would like to confront, to move from obsessions and compulsions to valued action in a particular domain. What would you like to practice confronting? Create a list of possibilities. You may find it useful to review your How Does OCD Impact Your Life?, Understanding Your Maintenance Cycle of OCD, and Values exercises to guide you.

Start listing situations you would like to confront. Next, for each situation, rate your distress level on a scale of 0 through 10, with 0 being no distress at all and 10 being the highest level of distress. Some people get stuck on choosing the "right" number. If this is true for you, simply rank your triggers at low, medium, or high levels.

With your ERP menu complete, you can choose a single step to begin with.

Exercise: Creating Your ERP Plan

Download the ERP Practice Diary form (available, with a completed example, at http://www.newharbinger.com/51024) or just follow the steps as you read each section. This form is divided into two sections: pre-exposure planning and post-exposure debriefing. Each time you work on a new ERP task from your menu, work through this form, or simply answer the six pre-exposure planning questions, do the ERP, and answer the three post-exposure debriefing questions.

Step 1: Begin by choosing an ERP target.

What exposure would you like to do? For example, Lilly's exposure target is contagion and contamination fears.

Following the SMART criteria for successful goal setting will increase the likelihood that you complete your ERP and recognize your progress:

Specific

Measurable

Achievable

Relevant

Time-bound

Here's how SMART works. To be clear about what you want to accomplish when setting your goals, be *specific* about what, where, who, and when by asking yourself *What do I want to accomplish?*

To make your goal *measurable*, ask yourself *How will I know I accomplished my goal?*

If your goal is not achievable, you will get extremely discouraged. It's great to be driven and enthusiastic to use ERP to loosen the grip OCD has on you. But it's important for your goal to be realistic as well as challenging. Ask yourself *Is the step I'm planning to take realistic?*

A goal is *relevant* if it aligns with your values. If the goal is irrelevant, you're unlikely to have the motivation to complete it. Ask yourself *Does my goal align with my values?*

A *time-bound* goal includes a specific time frame that is not too far into the future—preferably something achievable in the next week. Ask yourself *What time frame do I want to set for completing my goal?*

Now it's your turn to practice setting some SMART goals based on your ERP menu.

Step 2: What is your SMART goal?

You may want to choose something that you think will be more manageable for you, or something that currently is highly disruptive to your daily life that would be a priority to work on. It's crucial to choose an ERP task that you are 100-percent all-in with completing, meaning that you're willing to allow uncomfortable feelings to be there without trying to make them go away and without performing a compulsion afterward. If there are no tasks like that, break one of your current tasks into even smaller steps until you find one where you are 100-percent all-in.

For example, one of Lilly's ERP menu tasks, now modified to reflect SMART principles, is "I will sit outside on my back porch holding Rolph for ten minutes each evening for the next week, because I love my dog and it is a joy to have his companionship. My RP plan is to not take a shower until the following morning or to wash Rolph's feet. Instead, I will sip a cup of tea while visiting with my roommate."

To support learning, it is useful to identify what you fear will happen when you complete your ERP.

Step 3: What do you fear will happen when you complete your ERP?

When you consider this, also consider how likely it is that the outcome you fear may actually happen (0 to 100 percent).

For example, Lilly fears she and Rolph could unknowingly touch something dangerous on the ground and get sick or die. She could unknowingly cause harm to someone else by spreading something dangerous. Not knowing would be way too much to handle. Lilly estimates that it is 70 percent likely that they will encounter something on the ground and get sick from it.

Step 4: How has your OCD interfered with engaging in meaningful activities related to your goal?

For example, Lilly misses the companionship of her dog and the relaxation she experiences with walking for exercise.

Step 5: What values are related to your ERP goal?

Take a few minutes to slow down and describe what is important to you about your ERP goal. As you write, notice your emotions, bodily sensations, thoughts, and mental images.

Here is what Lilly wrote: "I love Rolph and miss walking him around our beautiful neighborhood. I love the twinkle in his eye and his excitement as I attach the leash to his collar. Just thinking of this, I feel sad and have a queasiness in my stomach. I want to be a good companion for my sweet dog."

Next, it is important that you have an RP plan that you intend to follow after completing your exposure. You will likely be tempted to avoid anxiety by performing a compulsion after completing your exposure task. This is expected, but to break free from your OCD cycle, you will need to follow your RP plan. This plan is simply a guide that you agree to follow when you are triggered after the exposure step of your ERP so that you don't do a compulsion. To determine your RP plan for a given task, ask yourself *When my obsession tells me to do a compulsion in this scenario, what will I do instead?*

Step 6: After completing your exposure task, how will you practice RP by not engaging in compulsions or avoidant behaviors?

For example, Lilly will find it difficult to not take a shower after going outside or to not wash Rolph's feet, in case he walked on dangerous ground without her knowing it. Her RP plan is to not shower or wash Rolph's feet after her exposure. Instead, Lilly plans to have a cup of tea with her roommate in the living room.

Now that you have done some good preparation for your ERP by understanding your OCD maintenance cycle, developing your ERP menu, and setting SMART goals, let's look at how to implement your ERP. First, we will look at Lilly's experience.

Implementing ERP

Prior to starting her exposure, Lilly reflected on what is important to her related to her ERP goal. As she opened the door to the back porch, her stomach felt queasy. As she sat with Rolph, she noticed that her anxiety was surprisingly variable over the ten-minute time period she had set.

The exposure was much easier than she had thought it would be. She discovered that her anticipatory anxiety was much worse than the actual exposure. Once she and Rolph settled into the chair, she enjoyed holding him. She had the thought *What if I lose him?* and immediately felt sad and anxious. Staying present to her internal experience helped her realize that feelings come and go. And in the end, she felt proud of herself for sticking with it. The exercise was demanding and challenging, while also rewarding.

Now it's your turn to implement ERP practice with a task that you are willing to do.

Exercise: Personal ERP Practice

Before practicing your exposure goal, take a moment to reflect on what is important to you about that goal. Notice your internal response while you reflect on this. Think about what your mind expects you to experience as a result of doing exposure.

Next, begin your exposure task and notice any thoughts, emotions, and sensations that you feel in your body. Stay with your task and observe your response. Don't fight your fear. You can learn to surf the ups and downs of your discomfort; just stay present and observe your experience while you complete your exposure task. If your mind starts looking for ways to avoid your discomfort, notice that and return to being present. It is common for your mind to mentally time travel with what-if scenarios about the future. If you notice this happening, direct your attention back to your exposure task.

As you're completing your exposure task, and afterward, follow your ERP plan so you are not performing compulsions. After you've completed an ERP practice, reflect on what you learned. Keeping a record of what happens using the ERP Practice Diary (a free tool available, with an example, at http://www .newharbinger.com/51024) will help you see patterns in your experience.

How did your practice with your first ERP task go? Remember, it doesn't matter how small your ERP goal was. ERP is challenging, and completing your goal is huge! Give yourself some credit, and don't discount your progress.

Once you complete your ERP task, reflect by answering the post-exposure debriefing questions on your ERP Practice Diary. This is an important step to help enhance your learning.

Exercise: Post-Exposure Debriefing

Describe what you experienced during and after completing your ERP. What did you learn from your experience? In what ways were you surprised?

It's important for you to make ERP practice part of your daily life. Plan ERP regularly and gradually work through the tasks that you listed on your ERP menu.

ERP in Daily Life

Targeted practice with ERP tasks is always helpful; it will also help you live more flexibly if you shape your routines to give you more opportunities to get out of your comfort zone. There will be times that you will encounter an unexpected trigger, and by creating and following your ERP plan, you can learn to respond to your OCD differently. Even if you take a very small step, creating a lifestyle where you regularly look at your responses to triggers and consciously change them will help you build the life you want to live.

Mae has moral scrupulosity obsessions. She enjoys going to Starbucks each morning for coffee and a breakfast treat. One of her favorite baristas was working, and while she waited for her coffee, they exchanged small talk. During their conversation, she had the urge to blurt out a racial slur—something that had never happened to her before. She immediately felt a surge of discomfort in her body as she tried to "figure out" whether she'd actually said it or not. She wanted to make statements such as "I'll bet you get offensive customers from time to time" to seek reassurance in a roundabout way. She also found herself wanting to watch his expressions carefully to see if he looked upset. This effort to "figure it out" and gain reassurance is a form of mental compulsion. For ERP, she chose to not engage in any reassurance-seeking behavior, either at Starbucks—where she just took her coffee with a smile and walked out, turning her attention to her environment rather than her OCD thoughts to ground herself— or for the rest of the day. She has practiced ERP so regularly that she's equipped to spontaneously do ERP even when her OCD finds new ways to express itself.

Now let's look at Sally's experience.

Sally's obsessions were related to a fear of HIV: I might get HIV and die *or* If I get HIV and don't know it, I could bleed and infect someone else who could die. *After a year of consistently practicing her ERP, the thoughts would still sometimes occur if she saw a used Band-Aid in a parking lot, for instance, or something that looked like it could be blood in a public bathroom—but she was able to respond differently to those thoughts. She would notice a twinge of discomfort and move on. Several years later, while traveling and pulling her luggage, she saw a brown spot on the ground and thought* Maybe that's blood. Maybe it has HIV. *When she arrived at her hotel and wiped off her bag, she thought* Maybe I unknowingly touched what might be blood and then touched my clothes. *She recognized this as an OCD moment and began planning ERP exercises she could do on the fly. For starters, she touched all her clothes to her face while unpacking. She touched her toothpaste and toothbrush and then brushed her teeth for exposure. Through it all, she was able to use her skills to stay free of the stickiness of OCD.*

How might you apply these examples of practicing ERP in your life?

Structure and Practice

In summary, you can maximize your success during exposure when you:

1. Plan your ERP using SMART goals aligned with your values.

2. Are all-in with your ERP practice.

3. Hold your values in your mind as you engage in ERP practice, so that you understand why you are choosing to do ERP.

4. Allow any thought, feeling, and sensation in your body to be there without fighting it during your exposure.

5. When you find yourself distracted, notice it, and return to staying present with your discomfort.

6. Don't engage in avoidance strategies that prevent you from staying present to your internal response to your fears.

7. Follow your RP plan.

8. Reflect on what you learned from your experience with ERP.

To accomplish your goals that help you live a meaningful life, you'll need to make progress through the tasks required to reach each goal, which means you'll need to consistently and persistently practice your ERP skills. Think of it this way: To play a wide repertoire of beautiful music on a wind instrument, a musician needs to practice scales, breathing exercises, vibrato exercises, and etudes that help them master certain technical skills. Practicing each skill makes it easier for them to enjoy playing the music they love. Practicing ERP is similar. There are a variety of skills, and when you put them all together, you can loosen the grip OCD has on you.

So far, you've learned how to create your ERP menu and SMART goals and implement situational ERP. You've also learned that consistent, intentional practice with situational ERP is important for your success in living a more flexible lifestyle. In the next chapter, you'll learn more of the skills that will help you practice ERP well. Specifically, you'll learn skills to break the rule that says *You must always control your internal experiences.*

CHAPTER 4

Practice Principles of Aikido

What might it mean for you to break the OCD rule that states *You must always control your internal experiences?* Internal experiences include all your thoughts, feelings, images, memories, and the sensations you feel in your body. When you try to control these experiences, you often end up in a battle with yourself. To resolve this battle, you can weaken what gives OCD power by finding your center, the place where you are present, open, and observant of your internal experiences. As you practice, you'll find that unwanted mental events are dynamic, as you observe them rise and fall just like waves in the ocean.

What Drives the *You Must Maintain Control* Rule

Resistance to suffering in our lives is a universal human experience. But what you resist gains strength, and the more you resist, the more exhausted you'll feel, and the more your life will feel limited. Struggling and fighting to control your anxiety keeps your energy focused on your uncomfortable internal experiences instead of on living life fully. This creates a paradox: Your attempts to maintain control of your internal experiences by following the rules of OCD create more of the very discomfort you want to avoid. Although making room for your inner experiences seems like the opposite of what you'd want to do, with practice you'll find that it's what is most effective.

To illustrate, let's look at my childhood encounter with a Chinese finger trap. My family was vacationing, and we went to a store that had a little bit of everything—souvenirs, trinkets, and games. I was curious about a basket of little straw tubes that you insert you fingers into. Of course I put my fingers in, and when I tried to get them out, I found that I couldn't. The tube was designed to keep my fingers locked into it. I was trapped! I did the natural thing and kept trying to escape by pulling my fingers apart. The more I pulled my fingers, the narrower the tube got, and the more stuck I became. It turned out that I needed to push my fingers *into* the tube so it would expand. Sometimes what seems to be a solution is the opposite of what you need to do.

How might this apply to your OCD? It's a way to understand the ERP principles we talked about last chapter. If you can push your fingers into the trap—deliberately do something that brings on anxiety—and learn to surf the discomfort that results, without giving in to compulsions, you can free yourself of OCD more effectively than you can if you give in to that urge to pull your fingers out. Even if, in the short term, your discomfort is greater than it would be if you did a compulsion.

All forms of resistance take you away from your center. Your center is a stance where you are aware, moment to moment, open to what shows up inside and curiously observing your internal experiences. When you are centered, you know what's important. From your center, you're in touch with your agency as you choose your behaviors with intention. Mindfulness, acceptance, curiosity, and knowing your values are essential practices that can keep you centered.

Mindfulness is present-moment awareness of internal feelings, thoughts, bodily sensations, and external observations. Deficits in mindfulness are common for anyone who suffers from OCD (Didonna et al.

2019). When you have an obsession, you may find yourself mentally time traveling to the future with a what-if thought or mentally reviewing a past event you have questions about. As this develops into a story—a narrative you consistently tell about yourself and come to believe—you may find yourself judging your thoughts as dangerous or important in some way. This keeps you off center as you go on autopilot, responding with compulsions or avoidance.

Nonacceptance of internal experiences is a core issue that can keep you struggling (Didonna 2009). When you get hooked by the content of your obsessions and interpret them as literally true, you may fight to push your discomfort away rather than embrace it as an internal event that you don't need to alter.

Feelings of discomfort are a natural part of being human and can give you important information. Your internal discomfort is not a problem to be solved. Applying problem-solving strategies and logic to your obsessions will simply exacerbate them.

Chances are you've had loved ones try to help you using logic and problem solving when your obsessions arise. For example, it's not uncommon to hear reassurances like "It's not possible for you to harm someone if you do something at a bad luck time," or "You only have to wash your hands for thirty seconds," or "You would definitely know if you'd hit someone while driving." Statements like these are well-meant and often lead to further efforts to convince you that your obsessions are irrational—which OCD will never really let you believe.

Of course, in ordinary life, problem-solving strategies are fantastic—say, if you need to resolve some scheduling conflicts, or if your car breaks down on the road. But when you apply these strategies to what goes on within you, they will exacerbate your struggle. Your anxiety is not a problem you can solve—but it's an internal experience that you can relate to differently, once you know to break free of the *I must maintain control* rule.

How This Rule Affects Your Life

You must always control your internal experiences affects everyone with OCD. Let's look at an example that demonstrates the consequences of just how insatiable OCD can be.

Juanita's Story

Juanita has an obsessive fear of mold growing in her house that could jeopardize her family's health. In response, she repeatedly checks her faucets before leaving home. On an average day, she takes about forty-five minutes to check each faucet by looking at it, tapping it, and stating out loud "It's off." As she moves through her day, she frequently mentally reviews the steps she took when leaving her home. On some days her anxiety becomes so intolerable that she returns home to check her faucets again.

Juanita plans to take her family on an enjoyable weekend getaway. She anticipates that her obsessions about the faucets being off will be stronger. When away from the house for a longer period of time, the stakes are higher if she's neglected to turn off the faucets. She takes photos with her phone so she can review it later as part of a reassurance compulsion to "make sure" she really shut the faucets off.

After traveling to their destination, her mind begins to obsess: What if I didn't check all the faucets? There could be a flood. *Juanita feels scared and shaky, so she grabs her phone and reviews her photos meticulously. After reviewing the photos, her mind says* Maybe the lighting in the photo isn't capturing the faucet in the right way to know if it's off. *She asks her family to look at the photos too, and they reassure her the faucets are off. Then her OCD insists* What if you went back after taking the photos, used the faucet, and neglected to turn it off? You could have forgotten to take a picture. *Each time, Juanita mentally reviews the steps she has taken—and once she feels a little relief, her OCD has a response that creates more anxiety. As she struggles with her obsessions, she has difficulty engaging in fun activities with her family.*

Juanita is hooked by the content of her thoughts. And each time she checks her photos and mentally reviews the steps to get relief, her mind generates more questions to be concerned about. Juanita notices that she has further questions that create anxiety rather than the peace of mind she wanted.

In this example, we can see that as Juanita has anticipated what she might worry about and applied a problem-solving strategy. But what seemed to be a logical solution to control anxiety by taking photos of the faucets backfired: it only created more obsessions and compulsions. She hasn't yet realized that the problem is in the way she's engaging with her obsessions—by embracing them, then trying to avoid the internal discomfort they cause.

There are many ways you may avoid the internal discomfort created by OCD. Other common control strategies include procrastination, distraction, substance abuse, and too much screen time.

Exercise: The Control Rule

Reflect on how you follow the rule *You must control your internal experiences* by identifying specific thoughts, compulsions, and avoidant behavior that you engage in. How does following this rule affect your quality of life and limit your pursuing what matters to you?

Now that you know the signs that indicate you're following this rule, we'll address how you can break it.

Breaking Free

Freeing yourself from this rule requires changing your relationship with your discomfort so you can create flexible behavioral responses that promote living life fully, no matter what your brain is throwing at you. To respond more effectively, it will help for you to practice three skills: present-moment centering with a curious attitude, acceptance, and knowing your values. Centering yourself in the present moment and approaching your own experience with curiosity allows you to accept it and avoid fighting it with avoidance and compulsions; knowing your values will give you a sense of which actions to take instead so you can live life as *you* want to live it.

Aikido, a Japanese martial art, includes principles that will help you put these skills into practice. Aikidoists welcome their opponent and view this as an opportunity to learn. When you have a disturbing obsession, you can say: *Yes, bring it on. I welcome this opportunity to learn.* It might sound wild now, but saying yes in this way can promote curiosity as you open up flexibly to new experiences in your life, even if you feel uncomfortable.

In the practice of aikido, the attitude toward oneself and one's opponents is one of respect and care. Practitioners emphasize not allowing harm to their opponent. It is understandable that you may not want to treat your OCD with respect and care, but keep in mind that your OCD is part of your own brain that is overworking in its efforts to keep you safe. Using mindfulness and acceptance, you can practice noticing the dynamic nature of your disturbing thoughts as they rise and fall.

Imagine an opponent moving toward you to throw a punch. Your natural response might be to get ready to throw a punch yourself or to run away. In aikido, action is focused on redirecting the energy of the opponent rather than resisting it. In contrast to a face-to-face punch by an attacker, aikidoists execute spherical movements where they maintain balance and an optimal distance as they redirect the momentum of their attacker, which will throw them off balance. As aikidoists move in this way, their opponent isn't directly face to face, because they will pivot off the opponent's path. For example, a 180-degree pivot will leave you shoulder to shoulder moving in the same direction as your opponent. You may have the urge to do whatever your mind tells you so you can get temporary relief. A 180-degree pivot in your mind will involve doing the opposite of what your anxiety wants you to do. Remember, it is not the experience of anxiety that is the problem; it is your response to it. By pivoting in this way, the opponent has nothing to resist against. You can learn to respond to your OCD so that you leave it with nothing to resist against.

For example, in response to an obsession like *If you don't check, someone will get hurt,* you can say *Thank you, OCD. I know you are just trying to help keep people safe. I've got this. Off to work we go.* You are in charge and can walk side by side with your OCD as you go through your day. If you intentionally invite it along, it has nothing to resist. If you don't, anxiety feeds on your resistance to it, or your unthinking accommodation of it, both of which allow it to generate new worries and fears.

Responding in this way to your relationship with your discomfort won't feel natural at first. But with practice, you'll find that fighting with discomfort takes more time and energy compared to practicing the principles of aikido. And when you welcome the anxiety that you feel in response to your obsession, you are taking charge of your response rather than reacting in a way meant to stop your discomfort. Treating the side of your mind that is anxious with care and respect, being able to mentally step back and notice thoughts without judging them, takes power away from your disturbing thoughts and gives you space to live the way that *you,* not your OCD, want to live.

Curiosity

An attitude of curiosity is an innate, natural, and powerful trait (Brewer 2021). It creates openness to new experiences and promotes your growth by allowing you to explore and discover new things. When this is satisfying, you are more likely to repeat it and develop skills that expand your life experiences (Kashdan 2009).

What would happen if you brought curiosity, rather than resistance, to the experiences that trigger your OCD? Let's consider two stances you can take when planning to venture out of your comfort zone by doing something important even while you are anxious. You may approach the thing you're about to do with thoughts like *What if something terrible happens? I'm already feeling panicky, so maybe I can't handle my anxiety. My OCD is probably going to beat me up.* You could also approach it with curiosity, like *Hmmm, I wonder what will happen if I do X? Let's see what happens when I do something even while I'm anxious.* Which one will help motivate you to explore? Seek out opportunities to practice approaching life with curiosity.

Exercise: Take a Curiosity Walk

Take a walk outside and look for something that you have not noticed before. Notice how many shades of color you see in foliage or objects. What is the most distant sound you hear? What is the smallest thing you can see? What shapes can you see in between objects? What is your experience with each footfall? Does one step feel heavier than the other? Be curious about what you notice. Did you notice anything new? What emotions did you have during your walk? Try noting these in your journal.

Doing exercises like this can help you cultivate curiosity and create openness to exploring new experiences. Curiosity promotes willingness to discover what works even while you're anxious.

Willingness and Acceptance

Willingness and acceptance are critically important to effectively practicing ERP. Much as an aikidoist mentally says yes to their opponents, you can willingly accept inner experiences that you have been avoiding. Simply put, you purposely make a choice to be willing to stay present with all your feelings, thoughts, and bodily sensations without the intent to make them go away. The anxiety you feel in response to your obsessions can feel so intense and huge—so huge it feels bigger than life. But as you practice allowing you inner experiences to come and go, you'll find that your internal reactions to your obsessions are not as big as you anticipate. And as long as you're willing to stay with them long enough, *without* resorting to compulsions, the intensity will subside into something you can handle.

Let's try a quick exercise to help you start working with sensations in this way.

Exercise: Noticing Uncomfortable Sensations

For this exercise, you'll need a couple of pieces of ice and a towel for the water as the ice melts. Hold the ice in the palm of your hand and notice your thoughts, feelings, and sensations in your body as they change, moment to moment, without judging your experience. How does the ice feel in your hand? What does your mind do when the sensation becomes uncomfortable? How does your body want to respond?

Notice any desire or attempts to try to control your experience. Do you want to throw the ice away or change hands? Do you grit your teeth or close your eyes? Practice allowing your experiences to come and go. Caution: After the exercise, take care to check the floor and sponge up any melted water.

In your journal, write down your reflections on your experience during this exercise. What was it like to observe your experience without changing it? What did your mind want to do to eliminate your discomfort?

With this exercise, you practice approaching discomfort with curiosity by observing your internal experiences without judging or getting hooked by them. Noticing and accepting your discomfort as it comes and goes is exactly what you are practicing when you do ERP.

Willingness and acceptance are necessary for you to be 100-percent all-in with facing your fears. Another necessary skill for this learning process is to practice mindfulness, so you are fully present with what each moment has to offer.

Mindfulness

Practicing a variety of mindfulness skills regularly will help enhance your ERP by allowing you to notice the space between your obsessions and how you respond, so you can choose a direction you want to go in. Over time, you'll likely find present-moment awareness enriching to your everyday life too.

There are a variety of ways to practice mindfulness. Some are very informal, such as being aware of sensations while taking a walk or doing a chore; others are more formal, such as developing a consistent meditation practice. Research has shown that mindfulness practices have health benefits including reduced stress levels. The following are some informal mindfulness practices that can help you stay present, along with an exercise that will help you practice staying mindful even when compulsions arise. Practicing mindfulness will help build your capacity to tolerate your discomfort.

For best results, establish a daily practice of at least one informal mindfulness activity. All the practices that follow can help you to stay in the moment with what you are experiencing. Each time you notice your mind time traveling out of the present moment, you'll simply acknowledge this and return to the moment. Do this without judging your mind or telling yourself stories about the experience. Simply refocus on the present moment each time you notice your mind drifting off to the past or the future.

After each exercise, reflect on your experience. Is it different from your usual experience? Did your perception of the passage of time change? Did anything stand out? What was your mind doing? What did you learn from your experience? Did your attitude change about the task you chose?

Did your mind try to fight your experience by rushing, getting impatient, or attempting to multitask?

Practice the following mindfulness exercises with curiosity and choose some that you can do each day to build your skills. Don't be surprised if you find mindfulness exercises challenging—everyone experiences that. It's important to choose a practice you'll do regularly, then stay patient and willing to commit to the practice, even on days when it's challenging or when progress feels slow.

Exercise: Mindfulness with a Small Object

Choose an object to look at curiously. For example, you might think *Hmmm, I wonder how many shades of color I can see? I wonder how it feels to touch different parts of it? I wonder what it sounds like if I tap it in different areas?*

Reflect on your experience and write in your journal. This is good practice for applying these questions to your daily mindfulness practice.

Exercise: Mindfulness During Routine Activities

Choose an activity that you do regularly. It could be taking a shower, brushing your teeth, combing your hair, or anything else you do regularly. For instance, say you choose brushing your teeth as your activity. Every time you brush your teeth, practice being in the present moment. Notice the color of your toothpaste and toothbrush as you move the toothbrush to your teeth. What do you notice next? Notice the sounds of water and of the toothbrush scrubbing your teeth. What tastes and smells do you notice? What internal experiences show up as you are brushing your teeth? Where does your mind go? Do you notice any emotions? What is it like to notice the sensations in other parts of your body while brushing your teeth? Just notice your experience. As you notice your mind traveling to the past or future, return to the present moment.

Mindfulness during chores. Choose a chore that is a nuisance to you and pay attention to it with your five senses. What do you see as you are performing the chore? What do you hear? What sensations do you feel while doing your chore? Is there a smell or a taste? Did you notice yourself getting distracted? What was your mind thinking? Each time you notice yourself thinking of anything besides the chore, gently return to awareness of your present-moment experience of doing the chore.

Mindfulness while waiting. When you find yourself in line at the grocery store, waiting for a train, or driving in traffic, stay present with your five senses and notice what your mind does.

Mindful walking. While taking a walk, notice your breathing and the sensation of the soles of your feet as you take each step. As you observe your mind wandering, just notice kindly and return to your breathing and the soles of your feet.

Mindful listening. Choose a song or an instrumental composition to listen to in a variety of ways, and be curious about what you experience. For example, *Hmmm, I wonder what it will be like if I listen to this focusing only on the percussion, or the lyrics?* The idea here is to experience a piece of music in different ways by focusing on one instrument. What did you notice? When you focused on different instruments in the music you chose, did it change your experience with it? Did it change your usual experience when you listen to the music?

Mindful eating. Slow down while you eat and stay present in your experience with each bite and notice the spaces in between.

Exercise: Mindful Meditation

Here you'll find guidance for a more formal mindfulness practice. Begin with sitting comfortably upright and set a timer for one minute. Close your eyes and notice your breathing as you take each breath. If your mind or anything in your environment distracts you from focusing on your breath, kindly notice it and return back to your breath.

One minute of time is a reasonable place to begin when you're first starting out with mindfulness practice. I suggest taking a few breaks in your day to do a one-minute mindful meditation and noticing what it's like. If you are willing to continue gradually lengthening your time of practice—say by a minute or so, every few weeks, until you're regularly setting your timer for fifteen minutes—you'll likely find it beneficial in your practice of being present.

Exercise: Mindfulness During a Compulsion

As you go through your day, you may notice some compulsions that you are ambivalent about stopping. If this is the case, practice your compulsion mindfully by staying present to your experience. For example, if you have compulsions to decontaminate that take an excessive amount of time, notice what it is like to stay present with it using your five senses. If you are washing your hands, what does it feel like as you go through the steps of your compulsion? Are your hands feeling tired or raw? Is the soap irritating your skin? What does your mind do during the compulsion? Notice what you learn from this and whether it changes your willingness to use ERP.

Staying present to your experience during ERP is critically important for you to gain maximum benefit. In this way, mindfulness skills, which teach us how to be present with what we experience without judgment of it, will enhance your practice of ERP. What's more, your habits of avoiding what triggers your anxiety and performing compulsions can be so automatic that you may not recognize that you have a choice. Developing mindfulness skills can help you notice the space between your trigger, your obsessions, and your compulsions in real time. By staying present, you can learn to briefly pause, redirect yourself in a more productive direction, pivot, and proceed in the new direction. Learning skills to notice, observe, and be curious about your internal experiences can help boost the effectiveness of ERP.

Paying attention, moment to moment, can help you notice when you are engaged in mental time travel. Unhelpful mental time travel about the future may contribute to worry about what can go wrong. A thought that begins with *what if* can get you hooked in an OCD story. You may also find your mind time traveling to past events to determine how you can avoid your anxiety. Mentally reviewing past events can become a mental compulsion.

For more information on mindfulness and how you can develop a consistent practice of it for your OCD, you might consult *Everyday Mindfulness for OCD* by Hershfield and Nicely (2017).

Juanita's Story, Revisited

Let's take a look at how Juanita worked through her struggle while out of town with her family. Juanita, wrung out by her worries about the faucets, tells her family she wants to return home. Then, using her newly acquired skills of present-moment awareness and observation, she sees the disappointment on her children's faces. She reflects on her experience and notices that she is trying to avoid feeling afraid by doing compulsions—her OCD is in charge. "Okay," she tells her kids. "Let's stay a little longer."

As her OCD generates another what-if scenario, she responds with Thanks, OCD. I know you are trying to keep me and my family safe. But I've got this. *She practices centering herself in the present moment by feeling the soles of her feet on the ground and noticing where she feels the anxiety in her body. She stays with her discomfort while noticing with curiosity.* I wonder what will happen as I stay with my discomfort for the next two minutes? *She allows her anxiety to be there without trying to change it. She notices her heart beating faster and feeling a rush in her stomach. She works to welcome this experience with the thought* Yes, this is a wonderful opportunity to learn. I want to enjoy my family even if that means my OCD has come along for the ride. *And with this, Juanita brings in her values— her love of her family and her desire to be a good parent who is present and enjoys time with her family. Rather than responding to her obsessions in a literal way and returning home, Juanita pivots toward interacting with her family and enjoying the rest of the weekend while feeling moments of anxiety. Once she changes her stance, she leaves OCD nothing to resist against.*

Points to Remember

As with aikido practice, you can separate the skills that will allow you to live free from your OCD, then combine any of them based on the situation:

- Knowing your center by practicing willingness and acceptance will help you say yes to living life more flexibly rather than getting stuck in compulsions and avoidant behaviors.

- Mindfulness practice will help you watch your inner experiences come and go in the present moment so you can do effective ERP and begin noticing the space between your obsessions and compulsions so you can choose what direction you want to go in.

- Approaching life with curiosity can promote creativity so you can make choices to live life more flexibly.

These are also ingredients for successful ERP. Just as the aikidoist uses fluid motions that redirects energy, you can move your energy toward what matters most—your values—even when you are anxious.

These challenging skills are ones we'll all practice for our whole lives. We are each a work in progress. Breaking rule one—*I must always control my internal experiences*—is essential for you to succeed in breaking all the rules of OCD. You'll notice that you'll use these skills as you work through this book. And as you add more skills to break each rule, you'll find that the fundamentals are practicing curiosity, openness, and present-moment centering. In the next chapter, you'll apply what you learned so far to breaking rule number two: *You must be absolutely certain.*

CHAPTER 5

Develop Your "Don't Know" Mind

In this chapter, we will address how to break the OCD rule *You must be absolutely certain*. Intolerance of uncertainty and doubt are core features that help keep you in your OCD maintenance cycle. When you find yourself trying to answer questions in your mind so you can "be sure," you'll find yourself experiencing more uncertainty. So you engage in a variety of time-consuming compulsions that involve reassurance seeking, checking, and avoiding situations that trigger your doubts.

You can learn how to allow uncertainty and ambiguity to be present by developing a "don't know" mind.

What Drives The *Intolerance of Uncertainty* Rule

We all live with uncertainty in our lives. Much of it we resolve automatically, such as with the assumption that loved ones we spoke to recently are safe, or that we'll have an uneventful experience running errands. Do we really know for sure? Can we really know what will happen from one moment to the next? The answer is no, we really can't know for sure, but we generally *assume* that we are safe enough when there are no signs of danger. Unless, of course, we have OCD—in which case we might find it incredibly difficult to tolerate uncertainty related to the obsessions that maintain our OCD cycle.

Intolerance of uncertainty is associated with OCD and anxiety disorders. Three types of uncertainty-related beliefs are described as important in OCD: (1) beliefs that it is necessary to be certain, (2) beliefs that you are unable to cope with unpredictable change, and (3) beliefs that you can't tolerate ambiguous situations—meaning the potential outcome is unclear (Taylor 2002). When you believe that your experiences associated with uncertainty are unmanageable, you respond to your obsessions with compulsive behavior as you try desperately to know for sure.

How does the normal experience of uncertainty, doubt, ambiguity, and unpredictability that everyone lives with become OCD? Intolerance of uncertainty is often associated with a pattern of overestimating threats. When you have OCD, your brain is extremely sensitive to perceived threats. When you are afraid of uncertainty, your threat system is easily activated "to be on the safe side." As with any threat, your focus becomes narrowed to assess the situation. As your focus narrows, you are processing limited information, so you start jumping to conclusions based on thoughts you associate with the threat. Once you think *what if*, a threatening story begins to emerge. This can create physiological distress—a relentless drive, in your mind, to solve the what-if story by "figuring it out" with additional information—which further reinforces your belief that "not knowing" may be dangerous. You might also start to avoid ambiguous situations. This provides temporary relief from anxiety, as you have an illusion of certainty. But it doesn't take long for your mind to generate another what-if question. The more you engage in ways to "be sure," the more uncertain you become, and the narrower and more constricted your life becomes.

The more you seek relief from your fear of uncertainty, the less confident you will be in your ability to assess your situation. Research has shown that repeated engagement in checking compulsions leads to memory distrust (Radomsky et al. 2014). More doubts about the accuracy of your memory just further validate that you can't trust yourself.

Intolerance of uncertainty is also linked to indecisiveness. It may seem like you can never gather enough information to make a good decision. There are often many equally good decisions to choose from and no one "best" choice. And although you can eliminate what would be undesirable choices, you can't know for sure which decision would be best. You can never know whether your decision has provided you with the best, second best, okay, mediocre, or worst outcome. When making decisions, you may experience analysis paralysis. You also lose out on opportunities to learn through experience that you can handle the things that happen to you, even when your choice in a given situation isn't the "best" one.

How This Rule Affects Your Life

You must be absolutely certain is a rule that affects almost every theme of OCD. Here are a few examples of the fears that can arise and the compulsions that can result:

- Fear of writing a curse word in an email, and checking repeatedly for inappropriate words to "be sure"

- Fear of purposely trying to sexually arouse someone after a party and mentally reviewing the event to "be sure"

- Fear of hitting someone while driving, circling around to check, and later watching the news

- Concern about being contaminated by a poisonous substance that causes a medical illness, then getting lost in excessive googling to gain information

- Asking loved ones for reassurance that you closed the garage door before you drove away, even though you already checked several times

- Wanting to make the "right" decision or risk being unhappy, and seeking reassurance from others

- Questioning whether you married the right person for you

- Questioning your sexual orientation and doing online searches for information to "figure it out"

- Wanting to know for sure whether you will go to heaven

Now that we have explored how your attempts to be absolutely certain keep you in your OCD maintenance cycle, you can begin identifying your own personal experience of following this rule. Signs include:

- Feeling fears around uncertainty, doubt, and the unknown

- Trying to eliminate doubt through certainty-seeking behaviors—like checking, gathering information, seeking reassurance—and covert mental compulsions, like reviewing events to alleviate your doubts about them

These, of course, only lead to *more* thoughts of doubt. You likely become less confident, which in turn can drive more compulsions. Ultimately, your avoidance of ambiguous situations, decision making, or situations with unknown outcomes contribute to your being stuck in the OCD maintenance cycle.

Exercise: The Certainty Rule

Reflect on how you follow the rule *You must be absolutely certain* by identifying specific thoughts, compulsions, and avoidant behavior that you engage in. How does following this rule affect your quality of life and your carrying out behaviors that matter to you?

Now that you know the signs that you follow the rule *You must be absolutely certain*, we'll address how you can break it.

Accepting Uncertainty

As you go through your life with a disorder that has been called the "doubting disease," it is important to be open to accepting uncertainty as a fact of life. This means facing the reality that we all live in: It is not possible to be 100-percent certain of safety in *anything*. Accepting uncertainty is instrumental to your breaking free from the hold OCD has on you. By now you know from experience that your desire to know and the compulsions that follow don't give you the control over the uncontrollable that you seek. It can't be denied that the adventure of allowing yourself to be uncertain, to not know, can be stressful, even painful. *And* it can open up exciting experiences in life that will be unavailable to you if you continue to seek certainty. Ultimately, the choice is yours—you can continue to be stuck in compulsions to try and be 100-percent sure, or you can open your life to possibilities by accepting uncertainty.

Sally's Story

Remember Sally? While walking to work, she noticed a Band-Aid on the ground. Although blood was not visible, her mind started wondering if she would contract HIV. As she went through the day, she found herself distracted with thoughts like Maybe that Band-Aid was bloody and I got it on my shoe. *She started mentally reviewing her actions and checked her shoe for signs of blood. Even though she didn't see anything, she found herself wondering whether she'd touched her shoe even though she didn't remember touching it. To be on the safe side, she carefully boxed up her shoes and put them in the trash.*

Ultimately, Sally felt like she couldn't bear the thought that she could unknowingly contract HIV and spread it to others. She got tested for HIV and was relieved to have a negative result. But after a short while, she began asking herself whether her results might've been mixed up with another person's. Her obsession continued, so she repeated the test again and again. The temporary relief she experienced with each negative test result did nothing to stop her need to be 100-percent certain. Her drive for certainty was insatiable; her mind creatively made up more what-if scenarios. Sally began avoiding friends, family, and activities to be on the safe side.

For Sally to succeed with ERP for her contamination obsessions, she must accept that the possibility of being 100-percent certain about anything is an illusion (Grayson 2014). She must accept the dire possibility that her OCD is stuck on—that she's had a false negative test result and could unknowingly spread HIV to people she cares about—and learn to live with that possibility as a remote one. This is an extremely crucial and challenging step for her. Her mind is insatiable as she tries to "be sure" so she will feel less anxious. But as you know from what you learned about acceptance last chapter, if she can accept the possibility, and the anxiety, without letting it control her behavior, she has a chance of breaking free.

One way you can shift your mindset is to draft an "acceptance of uncertainty" script: a script you can say to yourself to help support and strengthen you in the moments you're working to exercise your personal agency and actively break the rule *You must be absolutely certain*. Writing, hearing, and reading your acceptance of uncertainty script will remind you that experiencing uncertainty is a fact of life. This is the first step toward teaching your brain that experiencing uncertainty is not dangerous.

Sally wrote the following acceptance of uncertainty script that she posted on her kitchen refrigerator as a reminder to read it every morning:

I am afraid that I may have HIV and unknowingly spread it to others. I can't bear the thought that I could be responsible for another person's suffering. I have repeatedly been tested, spoken to my doctor numerous times, mentally reviewed my actions after seeing the Band-Aid on the street, searched the internet for answers, and isolated myself from people and activities I care about. None of these actions offered me more than a few moments of relief. I was tricked by my own brain to believe I could achieve certainty. The fact is, nobody can be 100-percent sure of safety. Living with uncertainty and risk is part of life for everyone, including me. So I accept that I will never know with 100-percent certainty whether all the HIV tests were accurate or not. And I accept that I will never know with 100-percent certainty that I don't have HIV. I also accept that I could unknowingly harm someone. That's a risk that's part of life. It is important to me to have close relationships and meaningful activities in my life, so I am choosing to live with this uncertainty while I pursue living the life I want. For me, this means that when I do activities with my loved ones, I will likely have thoughts, feelings, and sensations that are distressing. I can either live life with uncertainty or stay stuck trying to eliminate all risks by achieving certainty, which is impossible.

Exercise: Acceptance of Uncertainty Script

Write a script following the format shown (adapted from Hershfield and Corboy 2020). As you write your script, practice staying in the moment with your thoughts, feelings, and sensations as they arise.

Make sure you include the following information, and throughout the script include statements about living with uncertainty:

1. Briefly describe your OCD theme.

2. Describe how you follow the rule *You must be absolutely certain*.

3. What have you missed because of your OCD?

4. Provide some examples of behaviors that matter to you.

When you're done, take a moment to reflect. You just took a huge step by writing your acceptance of uncertainty script! What was it like? Did you find you could navigate the sensations that arose with mindfulness—and that while this may have been difficult at certain moments, it *was* possible?

Once you've written your script, there are a variety of ways you can use it. When you're just getting started on making this crucial shift in your mind to accept uncertainty, try to review your script as often as you can. Sally finds it helpful to read her script each morning to ground herself for the day. Posting it on the refrigerator door serves as a nice reminder whenever she's in her kitchen. Others like to post it on their bathroom mirror or keep it in their wallet.

You can listen to your script by reading it out loud or recording it in your own voice and playing it back. It is helpful to listen to it repeatedly while you reflect on its meaning. Listen mindfully, noticing your thoughts, feelings, and sensations.

Another listening strategy is to listen passively by setting your recording device on a loop so it will continuously repeat (Grayson 2014). Keep your sound level low and wear headphones while listening throughout the day. Of course, you'll need to switch it off when you need to concentrate and be fully present to other activities.

In the sections to come, I'll walk you through a number of other skills you can use to accept uncertainty and avoid defaulting to the compulsions your OCD pressures you to practice when you face uncertainty. These include mindfulness, learning when and how to make the bet that what your OCD is telling you is merited or not, and learning how to avoid the reassurance-seeking strategies you might default to in a bid to gain certainty.

Tapping into Your "Don't Know" Mind

Accepting that you can't ever be 100-percent sure means you can allow yourself to have questions that remain unanswered. Rather than trying to mentally figure out your mind's emotionally charged what-if questions, you can develop a *"don't know" mind*. When your threat-sensitive mind says what if, your problem-solving mind will want to answer the questions to feel relief from uncertainty-related fears. Rather than engaging in a compulsion, respond with *I'm going to allow this question to remain unanswered. I don't know.* Although this is likely to be emotionally charged at first, remember your mindfulness skills: Stay with your internal experience and observe how your experience changes. If you do this, you'll learn you *can* in fact handle whatever you're feeling without resorting to compulsions.

Freedom means allowing yourself to experience all the thoughts, feelings, and sensations that go with uncertainty. A "don't know" mind is not driven to find the answers; it is open to possibilities. To achieve freedom from following the *You must be absolutely certain* rule, you'll begin allowing yourself to leave questions unanswered. And a state of mind that embraces not knowing invites opening to a more flexible way of thinking and behaving. *I don't know* is a stance free of rigid thinking and beliefs, and following rules. Developing a "don't know" mind offers you possibilities that can become an amazing adventure.

Again, the main way to inhabit your "don't know" mind is to be mindful—especially in the moments your OCD and its need to be certain are triggered by uncertainty. When Sally wants to socialize, for instance, she may have triggering questions about her HIV status. Sally's problem-solving mind will want to search for the answer to these unanswerable what-if questions. Rather than engaging in a compulsion, she can pause, and say to herself *I'm going to leave that question unanswered. I don't know. I'm choosing to accept uncertainty so I can be a supportive friend and enjoy my social interactions.* As she moves moment by moment through her discomfort, Sally can notice and observe her internal experiences curiously, without judgment. And as she continues to practice her "don't know" mind, she will find that it's easier and easier to not get hooked into an exhausting compulsion to try and obtain certainty. Sally can stay with her uncomfortable experience while engaging in life activities of her choice rather than compulsions.

Exercise: Practice Your "Don't Know" Mind

Make a list of thoughts that give you a sense of urgency to find answers. After each thought, write "I'm going to allow that question to remain unanswered," or "I don't know." Stay in the moment and notice your experience as you practice using your "don't know" mind in response to each triggering thought.

Now that you have practiced using your "don't know" mind with your thoughts in a controlled context, you can use your mindfulness skills to attend to your five senses and to detect when you get hooked by your obsessions in the moment. If you get hooked, you may go on autopilot and perform a compulsion—just recognize that when you respond to your mind automatically in this way, you are missing out on key information that can help you move away from responding to your OCD with compulsions. Let's look at what mindfulness can make possible instead.

Five Senses Experiencing

Obsessions can create doubts about what you experience with your five senses.

Don may feel unsure of his five senses because of an uncomfortable physical sensation and a frightening story. Don's fear of something terrible happening is overriding his ability to trust what his five senses are experiencing. Let's look at Don's experience:

> I stand at each of my doors checking to make sure they are locked
> every time I leave my house and before bedtime. I jiggle it and hit it to
> make sure it's locked and then I still have doubts about it. I look to the
> left, look to the right, above and below the door, inspecting carefully
> to see if it is really locked. I'm almost positive it is, but I have my
> doubts. Something horrible could happen if someone came into the
> house at night. My children could be kidnapped, we could all get
> murdered, we could wake up to an empty house, and we could wake
> to someone bad holding us hostage. My mind goes wild with all these

horrific scenarios that could happen if I fail to lock the doors properly.
I couldn't live with myself if I was responsible for something terrible.

While Don is standing at his locked door, he is on autopilot, engaged in mental time travel to a tragic what-if story about the future. His mind is obsessing about something horrible happening to his family. When he focuses on his five-senses experience, though, he realizes that the more he checks, the more his body reacts—with his heart rate quickening, and uncomfortable sensations in his stomach—and the more his mind is stuck in the thought *Maybe the door isn't locked.* Notice what this actually means: During his checking compulsions, Don has actually become less confident that the door is really locked. There's a disconnect between what Don is thinking and what he can observe with his five senses. Even as he thinks *There's a chance the door could be unlocked—and something bad will happen!* he can *see* that the door is locked and *feel* that the door can't be opened.

This also means that in the end, Don can base his decision on mental time travel to the future about possible dangerous scenarios with an unlocked door, or he can use his five senses to help him assess the situation at his door in the present moment. You can learn to trust your senses instead of your obsessions by practicing using those senses and defaulting to making choices based on that information, while choosing to accept the residual uncertainty that your mind may get stuck on.

Trusting what you experience with your five senses over what your OCD tells you can feel like a huge risk. In those moments, you can practice an additional skill: making a hypothetical bet.

The Power of the Hypothetical Bet

Let's say you are in a position where you must make a high-stakes bet as to whether your fears merit attention or are based solely on OCD. Let's say in this what-if case, it's not just your own resources in jeopardy; your family's resources are too. These resources could include money, property, vehicles, and employment. Is your what-if story related to your OCD? You don't have the option to delay your answer. You must answer now. If the answer is yes, it's related to your OCD, take the chance that your fears may be correct and decide to stay with your uncertainty-related fears.

While Don is at the door checking, for instance, he can pause and get present by feeling the soles of his feet contacting the ground and noticing what he is experiencing with his five senses. Then he can make the bet that the what-ifs he's afraid of are just his OCD talking—and he can walk away from the door. It's another way to let acceptance do its work. In time, as he experiences the bets he makes as safe ones (they usually are), Don can develop a higher trust in his senses.

Once Don has made the bet and is willing to do ERP with his door-checking ritual, he can gradually decrease his checks. Earlier in this process, when he walks away from the door he will feel uncomfortable as he stays with whatever internal experiences he has moment to moment. This is challenging to do and takes repeated practice. But it can be done.

Can you think of a situation where you get hooked by your obsession and pay attention only to what your mind is saying? Next time that happens, feel the soles of your feet on the ground and attend to what your senses are telling you, moment to moment. Does that give you a broader perspective? What happens when you make a hypothetical bet?

Be aware that five senses experiencing and making a hypothetical bet can become compulsions. (See "Playing with Thoughts" in chapter 6.)

Next, you'll learn about a variety of ways that you may be seeking reassurance and how to do that less often—again, so you can learn to live with uncertainty rather than resorting to compulsions to try to eradicate it—which is impossible!

Reducing Reassurance Seeking

It is understandable that you would benefit from obtaining information in various ways to learn something important. Take OCD, for example. There are so many misconceptions about what OCD is and the best therapies to treat it. Learning about it from reputable sources can help you advocate for yourself and make important decisions that can help to free you from your OCD. But this can turn into yet another form of *unhelpful* reassurance seeking, like the kind you look for when your OCD pressures you to seek 100-percent certainty that an outcome you fear won't happen.

If your search for information on uncertainties you have is successful, once you have learned adequate information to satisfactorily settle the open question for the moment, you can move on to other activities, using the information you learned to guide you when needed. You'll also likely feel some satisfaction that you learned something that can help you. You may be curious and want to learn more, continuing to find your learning useful. Or you may find that the information you've gotten isn't enough to sate your fear of uncertainty—and you might feel compelled to dive still deeper and get still more information. In that case, you are engaging in a reassurance-seeking compulsion.

To make this distinction, look at what drives your behavior. Is it learning information that can help you, or distress when you want to *make sure* you know something without a doubt. When you have a relentless drive to answer questions in order to alleviate anxiety, you'll spend excessive time with your searches for "information," only to find that you are more afraid and confused, and your mind has generated more questions. Reassurance-seeking compulsions interfere with important areas of your life and take an excessive amount of time. As you move forward with breaking the rules of OCD, determine what is driving you to seek out information. Is it a desire to learn—or a desire to lower your anxiety? The first provides you with helpful information; the second leaves you stuck in your OCD cycle with more questions than you had to begin with.

There are several forms of reassurance-seeking compulsions that you may find yourself trapped in. Online searches for questions like "How can you tell if you are gay?" or "How do I know if I'm in the right relationship?" or "What does a tingly feeling in the head mean?"; reading articles or books or watching videos about the things you're afraid of—all of these can be ways of privately seeking answers to achieve certainty.

Mental compulsions can also be a form of self-reassurance. A mental compulsion is a behavior you use in your mind to "figure out" the answers to questions that you think will help you feel certain. This could be mentally reviewing past events in minute detail, making reassurance statements to yourself such as *door locked, stove off, lights off,* or repeating to yourself *It's okay, it's fine* like a mantra in response to something distressing.

Reassurance seeking often occurs with other people in your life. You may find yourself going to others for reassurance with direct questions such as "Did I shut the garage?" "Is this safe?" "Am I bad person for thinking this way?" or "Are you upset with me?"

Sometimes reassurance seeking can be more subtle, such as making statements and observing others for reactions. For example, let's say you drop a pen on the floor and are concerned about contamination. You may think that maybe you need to wash the pen and your hands just in case it picked up something contaminating on the floor. You could say "This is fine; I don't need to wash my hands" and observe how people react. If nobody is freaking out, then you may feel reassured. Confessing compulsions can be a form of reassurance seeking. A statement such as: "I just cursed at God" may get a response from your loved one like "God is good. He will forgive you," which can serve as a form of reassurance.

In their effort to give you support and ease your distress, people around you may unknowingly participate in your compulsions. We call this *cocompulsing.* And often, those who cocompulse with you aren't exactly thrilled about having to do it, even if they don't recognize it as cocompulsing per se. Research has found that relationship dissatisfaction can have a negative impact on your OCD (Abramowitz et al. 2013).

When Your Loved Ones Reassure You

For you to really learn how to live with uncertainty, it's important for people in your life to refrain from inadvertently cocompulsing. Chronic reassurance seeking can contribute to poor treatment outcomes and affect relationship satisfaction, as your OCD compulsions can be exhausting and frustrating for your loved ones as well. You can greatly enhance your progress with breaking the rules of OCD by asking your loved ones who accommodate and reassure you to gradually stop this behavior. To communicate this clearly, it can help to first write a letter explaining your most important discussion points.

Don's wife and children often reassure him just so they can move through their day more smoothly. For instance, Don's wife watches him lock the doors and reassures him that she saw the door locked when he moved away from it. She also takes photos of the doors in the locked position to reassure him so they can sleep at night. Don, knowing that this pattern will need to change if he's to break free of OCD, addressed his wife with a letter.

Dear Sadie,

I appreciate all the love and support you have given me over our life together. My OCD has been hard on all of us. For my health and the health of our family, I am working on breaking free from it. To do so, I am requesting your help. I have learned that my demand for reassurance by asking you to verify whether the door is locked is a compulsion that keeps me stuck. It is understandable that I would want reassurance when my OCD gets loud, and that when we are exhausted and need to go to bed, you would want to do whatever it takes to calm me down. But as we both know, the relief I get from your reassuring me is temporary. And I have learned that demanding reassurance from you is only making my OCD worse. I also know it's hurting our relationship: you feel burdened, and I stay uncertain and afraid, and that makes it harder for us to be close.

My goal is to gradually stop asking for reassurance that the doors are actually locked. To work on gradually eliminating my compulsion, I would like to limit myself to four reassurances for the day. I know that will be hard, and I also know that with your support, I can do it. I am going to keep track of it by having four coupons in my pocket. When

I ask you for reassurance, I will give you a coupon. Although I am committed to working on this, I may ask for additional reassurance. Please don't give it to me. Please respond with statements such as: "The most compassionate thing I can do for you now is to not answer your question. I can see you are struggling. And I know you've got this." I am hopeful that as we work together as a team, I can eventually eliminate my reassurance compulsions so that we can feel more rested, arrive to events on time, and have more time to enjoy our lives together.

If you'd like to write a letter to the loved ones who most often reassure you, guiding them in how they can help wean you off this compulsion, try writing one now.

Exercise: Letter to Your Loved Ones

Write a letter to your loved ones who give you reassurance. Begin with an expression of love and appreciation for them. Thank them for the support they provide to you. Next, give them information about your OCD and how you involve them. Make a request for their help. Describe your compulsion and how you want them to respond. Also, give them a heads-up on how you may behave when you want additional reassurance and guidance on how to respond when that happens. Close your letter with hopeful statements about what you are striving for that will have a positive effect on your relationship.

Instead of reassurance, your support person can give you truly supportive statements such as:

- If I do that for you, the OCD will get stronger.
- I can't offer you certainty. I don't know for certain.
- I've already answered that. Are you seeking reassurance?
- I want to be supportive of you, so I'm not going to reassure you.

As you saw in Don's letter, you and your loved ones can use tools to keep yourselves on track with your commitments to not seek or provide unhelpful reassurance. Two especially useful tactics are the reassurance coupons Don mentioned and a *reassurance book*.

Reassurance Book

With this tool, developed by Alec Pollard, rather than asking your loved ones for reassurance, you can write your question in a notebook you call the *reassurance book*, and wait a specified amount of time to look at the (one-sentence) answer that your loved one provides. This creates a delay in getting your reassurance, time that can help you learn to live with uncertainty. It also eliminates the conversation you may have with your loved ones where the two of you are cocompulsing.

Reassurance Coupons

Once you determine how many reassurances you want to use per day, you can make some coupons you can use to help you keep track. For example, if you want to limit your reassurance seeking to four times a day, you would commit to using only that many coupons. When you've used all four coupons, that's your last reassurance until the following day. Over time, you'll gradually reduce the coupon ration to zero as you eliminate reassurance seeking as a compulsion.

Practice Reminders

Develop some reminders that can help you anchor yourself in the reality that uncertainty is a fact of life we all live with. Be creative and develop some that have meaning for you. Here are some ideas:

- Write a reminder phrase on a sticky note. For example, if you engage in a lot of online search compulsions, or check compulsions with emails, you could post one on or near your computer.

- Draw a question mark or another meaningful symbol in a place you'll see it often that can regularly remind you to practice your "don't know" mind.

- Find an app that you can instruct to send you a text message or other notification with the specific message you know you need to hear about accepting uncertainty.

Exercise: Reminder Card

On an index card or something similar in size and shape, complete any or all of the following prompts to help you practice tapping into your "don't know" mind.

- Following the *You must be absolutely certain* rule has interfered in my life by: [whatever you are missing in your life by following this rule]

- The signs of following this rule include:

- I want to break the *You must be absolutely certain rule* so that I can:

- To break free from this rule, I will accept the reality that obtaining 100-percent certainty is impossible. I embrace the opportunity to accept uncertainty.

- I will intentionally do the following ERP tasks:

Points to Remember

We live with uncertainty every day of our lives. Uncertainty can activate your threat system unnecessarily. To be successful in living a flexible life with freedom from your OCD, you must accept uncertainty as a fact of life. Cocompulsing with loved ones can impede your progress. You can address this by involving your loved ones in your ERP plan, so they can help you stay on track with the task of resisting reassurance.

In this chapter, you've learned to interact with uncertainty differently—mindfully—using practices like writing an acceptance of uncertainty script, tapping into your "don't know" mind, using your five senses, making a bet with your OCD about likely outcomes and your ability to tolerate those outcomes, and learning ways to eliminate reassurance-seeking compulsions.

In the next chapter, you'll learn how to respond to your thoughts more flexibly so that you don't stay stuck in your OCD cycle.

CHAPTER 6

Think of a Pink Elephant

In this chapter, we will address how to break the OCD rule demanding that you *Pay attention to every single thought you have.* When you have OCD, thoughts that create anxiety are deemed to be significant or meaningful and become obsessions that intrude into your mind. It's natural to try to make the thoughts go away. However, as you've learned in previous chapters, the sensations you fight against rebound right back into your mind—often even stronger than before. In this chapter, you'll learn how to continue developing a healthier relationship with your thoughts so you can observe them for what they really are.

What Drives the *All Thoughts Are Important* Rule

Thinking is a natural process that occurs in your mind automatically. Your mind can have creative, helpful thoughts, and it can generate thoughts to help you anticipate danger—which can sometimes be helpful, and sometimes not. The range of content that your mind creates is not within your control. Historically, to stay safe, our ancestors reacted to danger forcefully—an overwhelming instinct to either fight whatever seemed threatening, to run to escape it, or to freeze in the hope it would go away. That instinct persists even now, but generally the threats we face aren't on nearly the same level as the ones our ancestors faced. Sometimes they're just imagined threats that our own minds generate. Still, your mind automatically categorizes experiences to keep you safe. And your brain often sends you thoughts that are disturbing and unhelpful, because it's wired to protect you from harm.

The human mind is also easily entangled with thoughts that are emotionally charged. Sometimes this may be adaptive: thoughts may promote safety or help you solve a problem. Other times, your thoughts are irrelevant, but when you treat irrelevant thoughts as important, this affects your behavior in ways that are unhelpful. When you focus on the content of your obsessions, you are misinterpreting mental noise as an important signal you must attend to (Wilson 2016). Of course, thoughts that help you solve real problems and keep you safe when you are actually in danger are signals you need to pay attention to. However, the content of your obsessions is, by definition, mental noise. They are a few of the many irrelevant thoughts that your mind generates.

Commonly held OCD-related beliefs that play a role in your following the *all thoughts are important* rule (Taylor 2002) include overvaluing the importance of thoughts, overvaluing the importance of controlling your thoughts, and overestimating threats. These beliefs leave you more vulnerable to having persistent unwanted thoughts.

Overvaluing the importance of thoughts is based on the distorted belief that all thoughts or images are significant in some way. An example, called *thought-action fusion*, occurs when you believe that when you have a "bad" thought, it is equal to a "bad" outcome; that a thought about immorality is equivalent to immoral behavior; or that thinking about something catastrophic will cause the feared event. In your mind, you may believe these thoughts say something terrible about who you are as a person.

Unwanted mental intrusions on violent or taboo obsessional themes are particularly painful and difficult to talk about. You may be relieved to know that research shows that over 90 percent of us humans experience unwanted intrusive thoughts or images (Abramowitz, Deacon, and Whitehead 2019). Scientific studies have examined the content of disturbing thoughts in both the general population and people with OCD. In one 1970s study, mental health professionals were given a list of unwanted thoughts from people without OCD and a list of obsessional thoughts from people with OCD—and they couldn't differentiate which thoughts belonged to which group (Rachman and DeSilva 1978).

Almost everyone reports having repugnant, unacceptable, violent, and taboo thoughts. Common unwanted thoughts include:

- Thoughts of pushing someone into traffic

- Thoughts of running the car off the road

- Impulses to yell a racial slur or curse at someone

- Impulses to throw something at someone

- Thoughts of harming a baby

- Thoughts of having sex with a relative

- Sexual thoughts about molesting a child

- Impulses to stare at someone's genitals (Baer 2001)

You may be wondering, though, why others around you don't seem to struggle with intrusive thoughts the way you do. For people who don't have OCD or anxiety disorders, intrusive thoughts pass through their minds and are not interpreted as important. If you have disturbing intrusive thoughts and you attach an important meaning to them, you pay more attention to them, falling into a trap of exhausting rituals. For example, you may try to mentally "figure out" whether you are dangerous or not. Questions such as *Am I a bad person?* or *Am I dangerous?* may lead to a variety of compulsions, such as finding ways to get reassurance.

Note that unwanted mental intrusions, as people with OCD experience them, are what we call *egodystonic*. This means you are having thoughts that are unacceptable and inconsistent with who you really are. Keep in mind, though, that having thoughts and urges is *not* equivalent to carrying out a behavior that you are against. Also keep in mind that the thoughts that grab your attention are the ones that attack the people and things you care about the most. (As a specialist in treating OCD, I have noticed that clients who have obsessions around violent and sexual themes are gentle, caring, and compassionate humans.) Above all, remember this: Having thoughts that feel unacceptable to you means nothing other than that you have a human brain.

When you overemphasize the importance of your thoughts, you'll most likely want to control them. Your mind may tell you that if you control your thoughts, you'll prevent negative outcomes. But as you've begun to learn, controlling thoughts is impossible—for anyone. And when you attempt to control your thoughts by trying to suppress or avoid them, these behaviors will, paradoxically, maintain the unwanted thoughts. The more you suppress your thoughts, the more frequent they will become, and because you are unable to get rid of the unwanted thoughts, you'll likely view them as more important (Wegner 1994).

To illustrate this, let's do an experiment. You'll need a piece of paper, a pencil, and a timer.

Exercise: Thought Suppression Experiment

Picture a pink elephant in your mind as you set a timer for five minutes. Now work very hard to not think or form any images of a pink elephant in your mind. Each time your mind sees an image or thinks of a pink elephant, place a mark on your paper.

What did you notice during this exercise?

When unwanted thoughts enter your mind, your automatic response is to suppress them, because the meaning you have attached to the thought is threatening and intolerable. But, as you just experienced in this exercise, when you try to keep a thought or image out of your mind, it actually causes you to pay more attention to it.

A counterintuitive response to unwanted intrusions—say, of pink elephants in your mind—is to allow yourself to think of pink elephants on purpose. That is, to let the pink elephant be there—even to welcome it in. In time, the intrusions will come and go less frequently.

Overestimating what you perceive to be threatening can drive the compulsions you perform so that you can feel safe. OCD-related thoughts are based on imagined threats to anything and anyone you care about.

When your mind interprets thoughts through a distorted lens based on these commonly held OCD beliefs, storylines develop. Your mind is a brilliant and creative storyteller—and when your stories are related to your OCD, your imagination can create elaborate, frightening worst-case scenarios.

Now that you have a better understanding of what drives this rule, let's look at how it might appear in your daily life.

How This Rule Affects Your Life

Following this rule leads you to become entangled in the content of your thoughts. Let's look at some examples:

- While attending a rooftop party, Candice was enjoying the beautiful view. A friend approached her, and suddenly Candice had a thought about pushing her off the building. She's since started questioning whether she cares for her friend and wondering if she unconsciously wants to harm her. And she now avoids both balconies and socializing.

- Tom was attending a worship service at church when he had an impulse to hit the person sitting in front of him with his Bible. Now, he's constantly mentally reviewing the service in his mind to reassure himself that he didn't do it, and he repeatedly asks his wife for reassurance.

- Beth was admiring her baby as she fed her. Then she had a thought about throwing the baby out the window. Now she questions whether she is a "fit" mother and fears that she is dangerous. She doesn't want to be alone with her baby and feels ashamed of this. When she has her disturbing thoughts, she says "not this, not this, not this" three times to erase it from her mind.

- Alexa is preparing dinner for her friends and family. As she cuts vegetables, a thought about stabbing her guests comes into her mind. She feels afraid and can't get the thought out of her mind. She moves her knives out of reach as she entertains her guests.

- Kim has a thought about touching their sibling's genitals as they play video games. They fear becoming a sexual predator.

When you follow this rule, you treat the content of your obsessions as a signal of something about you rather than the mental noise that it is. You find yourself taking the thoughts literally and doing something to make these thoughts go away, only to have them rebound in your mind—because, again, you're engaging them rather than letting them pass. You may find temporary relief by performing compulsions such as reassurance seeking, checking, or modifying your environment to create safety or avoid what triggers your thoughts.

Mental rituals are often used as a way of "undoing" thoughts or providing mental reassurance. Mental undoing rituals involve replacing bad thoughts with good thoughts, praying for safety, or changing the image to cancel it out. Phrases may be used to mentally erase the obsession, as Beth did with the phrase "not this, not this, not this." You may find yourself mentally reassuring yourself by reviewing each moment to determine whether you did something inappropriate, as Tom is doing, or attempt to mentally "figure out" whether you are dangerous or not. All these strategies often work only temporarily. And mental rituals keep you from engaging in your life with your five senses. When you do them, you are missing important information that can help you put things in perspective.

Sometimes people get confused about the difference between an obsession and a mental ritual. Remember: An obsession increases your anxiety, and mental rituals are your attempt to reduce anxiety.

Let's take a moment to reflect on your experience.

Exercise: The All Thoughts Are Important Rule

Reflect on how you follow the *all thoughts are important* rule by identifying specific thoughts, compulsions, and avoidant behavior you engage in. How does following this rule affect your quality of life and impact carrying out behaviors that matter to you? Picture your life without following this rule. What do you want to do differently?

Next, we will take a look at skills that will help you break free of this rule.

Breaking Free

To break this rule, your goal is to change your relationship with your thoughts so you can respond to them differently. Rather than viewing thoughts literally and thinking that the content means something about who you are, you can view them as temporary products of what your mind generates. When using ERP and ACT skills, you can experience your thoughts differently to loosen their grip on you. You can use mindfulness to approach your thoughts with curiosity, rather than instinctive defensiveness and resistance, and to identify when your OCD storyteller is providing you with noisy thoughts in real time. This will help you practice new ways of responding. Using imaginal exposure exercises in various ways can help you learn that thoughts are not dangerous. It is crucial to stop avoiding your thoughts for two reasons: when you avoid, you give them power, and you mistakenly view them as dangerous.

Use Your Observing Mind

We distinguish between two basic components of your mind: your thinking mind and your observing mind (Didonna 2020). Your thinking mind represents the part that generates all of your thoughts and images, regardless of the content. Again, thoughts are automatic, and much of what your mind generates is irrelevant to who you are as a person and what you find important in your daily life. Thoughts are simply temporary visitors in your mind.

Your observing mind does just that—it simply observes your internal experiences for what they are without trying to change them. Your observing mind is larger than your thinking mind; it offers a perspective that isn't defined by your thoughts, feelings, sensations, and memories. Think of your observing self as the constant sky and your thoughts, feelings, and sensations as the ever-changing weather. No matter how severe the weather is, it can't harm the sky (Harris 2009). When you observe your thoughts in this way, you can view them as temporary internal events that may or may not be useful. When your thoughts get loud and feel intense, stepping into your observing mind can keep you from getting entangled with them.

When you develop the ability to step into observing mind, rather than getting stuck in thinking mind, you have a strategy for those moments when OCD tries to trick you into thinking your obsession is an important signal. Your OCD storyteller views thoughts as literal, true, and important. If the story your mind has created gets you stuck and interferes with doing what is important to you, then treat it as a story—as weather that's passing through the sky of your mind. It can be useful to give the story a name, such as *There's the doom and gloom story again. I'm going to treat this as mental noise.*

Playing with Thoughts

This is a skill similar to using your observing mind, but one in which rather than engaging in behaviors to suppress your unwanted thoughts, you do a 180-degree pivot and welcome or invite your unwanted thoughts to be present. You have learned from your thought suppression experiment that when you try to push thoughts out of your mind, they rebound right back at you. What follows is a series of curiosity experiments that can help you form a different relationship with your thoughts, using your thinking mind in a way different from the way OCD pressures you to use it. Observe your experience curiously as you experiment.

Before you begin, one important caution: These exercises can be misused and become compulsions. The purpose of these ACT exercises is to develop a different, more flexible relationship with your thoughts. These exercises are not designed as anxiety-reduction techniques, nor are they intended to make fun of thoughts that are causing you distress. Be curious and notice how your mind responds to these exercises. There is no agenda for how you "should" respond. Just notice what it is like to experience your thoughts differently, and see whether any exercise is helpful for you.

- When an unwanted thought arises, add the sentence *I notice I'm having the thought that* [*fill in the thought*] or *I'm aware that I'm having the thought that* [*fill in the thought*].

- Vary the tempo of your thought. Say it so slowly that you can't recognize the thought or the words, and say it so fast that you get tongue-tied.

- Sing your thought to a familiar tune.

- Put a personality to your thought by using different voices—for example, cartoon voices, or the voices of characters in movies.

- Set your thought to a rap rhythm.

- If your thought was a character in an opera, what role would it take?

- Rearrange the words in your obsessions and state them out loud, or say the words backward.

- Write your thought on a card and carry it with you.

- Write your thoughts on sticky notes and post them around your home.

- Do an online search for word art generators and make word art with your thought.

- Make a collage of triggering words, phrases, or images.

- If your thought was an object, what would it look like?

- If your thought was on fancy paper, using fancy lettering, what would that look like?

Reflect on your experience with your thought curiosity experiments. What did you notice? Did working with your thoughts in this way help you see them differently—as mental phenomena that don't necessarily signal or say anything about you?

Experiment with these exercises regularly and see what happens. Does your experience with your thoughts change over time? Are you able to behave more flexibly in response to your thoughts?

Exposure to Thoughts

There are also various ERP exercises you can do with troublesome unwanted thoughts. The purpose of exposure to your triggering thoughts is to practice confronting your fear by purposely staying in contact with them, rather than avoiding or suppressing them. Exposure helps you learn that frightening thoughts are not dangerous.

If you have a fear of a particular word, number, or thought, it can be effective to repeat them on purpose: writing them on sticky notes and posting them where you will frequently see them, making a word art poster of words you are afraid of, and setting reminders to purposely think of the words, thoughts, or phrases.

One effective way to practice allowing thoughts to come and go without getting hooked by them is to make a recording of your triggering thoughts at various time intervals. Watching a timer, speak the thought for your recording and wait ten seconds, speak the thought again and wait thirty seconds, speak the thought again and wait five seconds. Vary the time up to ninety seconds and keep it as random as possible. For playback, wear a headset and listen at low volume during your day. When you hear your fear thoughts, simply notice them and move on. You can listen to your recording in this way for whatever time span you can manage. Start by experimenting with listening for one hour on a day and time that is most comfortable. Then try to establish a routine. At least one hour a day is fundamental; you'll gain even greater benefit by listening for longer periods, and eventually all day as you go about your usual routine.

As an ERP exercise, you can write an imaginary newspaper article about your experience of the feared event, or a screenplay. You could also take a real article related to your triggers and substitute your name in the article. If you are musically inclined, you can write a song that tells the story. If you are artistically inclined, drawing a story board of your script is extremely effective. You could also make a slide show that tells a story using images and words.

When you practice exposure to your disturbing thoughts, it can help you move through your day without engaging in them. When OCD says *You might hurt someone*, responses like *Duly noted*, *Maybe*, *I don't know*, *That's creative*, or *Thanks, I've got this* can keep you from getting hooked.

Points to Remember

Your mind generates thousands of automatic thoughts each day. When you look at your thoughts through the distorted lens of OCD, you'll feel threatened by them. Treating the content of your thoughts literally contributes to elaborate storytelling that keep you stuck in compulsions and avoidance. Attempting to control your thoughts, to no longer have the ones that bother you, is futile—but you can respond to them differently. You can form a new relationship with your obsessions by treating them as the mental noise they are and purposely allowing them to pass naturally through your mind. In this chapter, you've learned a variety of curiosity experiments and ways to use ERP for your thoughts to form a healthier relationship with them.

In the next chapter, you will learn skills to help you recognize false alarms, rather than automatically following the rule that states *The presence of any anxiety means you are in danger.* In addition to mental noise that occurs with thoughts, you'll learn to recognize body noise that can make your obsessions seem real.

CHAPTER 7

Recognize Your False Alarms

In this chapter, we will address how to break the OCD rule *The presence of any anxiety means you are in danger.* Your physiological responses can affect your behavior just as much as your thoughts and feelings can. When you have elevated anxiety sensitivity, you'll find yourself responding to sensations in your body as if they were signs of danger. In response to your obsessions, you may find that you experience physical sensations such as shakiness, rapid heartbeat, stomach upset, and hyperventilation. If you are hyperaware of an autonomic function such as breathing or swallowing, it's helpful to know that the uncomfortable sensations are not a problem, but your interpretation and the actions you take in response can create a problem. In this chapter, you'll learn about your body's natural responses to the perception of threat, how you can misinterpret these, and how you can coexist with your awareness, allowing the sensations to come and go.

What Drives the *Anxiety Means Danger* Rule

Anxiety sensitivity is essentially a fear of bodily sensations. Higher anxiety sensitivity is associated with OCD severity; it can impact your motivation to do ERP and interfere with your progress. Like much of OCD, it's a case of a normal, essential human function that becomes problematic.

Humans constantly process information from our physiological states—sensations, changes in bodily functions—and respond to it with behaviors. For example, if we haven't eaten in several hours, we feel sensations we associate with hunger, and we look for something to eat. While exercising outside on a hot day, we realize we're *too* hot and we slow down, take a break, get out of the sun, and drink liquids. This process is called *interoception*, and clearly it's essential to our survival. But with OCD, this process can work against us.

As a person with OCD, when you become anxious, you may feel sensations that are part of your fight-or-flight response system—an increased heart rate, butterflies in your stomach, rapid breathing, shakiness, light headedness and muscle tension, and more. These interoceptive cues are meant to provide important information that helps you maintain balance in your body, but OCD can also make them part of your OCD maintenance cycle. As you interpret sensations as dangerous, you engage in hyper-surveillance of your body. As a result, you notice the sensations more frequently and feel them more intensely when they arise.

When you interpret innocuous interoceptive cues as dangerous, your threat system may trigger your sympathetic nervous system with a fight-or-flight response to help you protect yourself. Your brain releases adrenaline and prepares your body to take action to keep you safe. And your body reprioritizes functions to get maximum energy to the parts that need it to take action quickly. Your breathing and heart rate accelerate to better deliver oxygen through your bloodstream to major limb muscles. As a result, you may feel breathlessness and chest tightness. Your blood supply to your head and extremities may decrease, to prioritize blood flow to the parts of the body that need it most—which can leave you feeling dizzy and lightheaded, with a feeling of unreality, and leave your hands and feet feeling cold. Your muscles can become tense, shaky, or even painful. To prevent your body from overheating, you may perspire. Your pupils dilate so you can see your surroundings better, but this may also leave you with unclear vision or light sensitivity. Digestion becomes a low priority, which can cause nausea and stomach discomfort. All of these changes can leave you with a dry mouth.

Again, this fight-or-flight response is the normal, adaptive, and efficient way the human body responds to threats. Unfortunately, your OCD predisposes you to respond more strongly than most to threats—which are often false alarms: perceived threats rather than actual ones. So your body is likely responding unnecessarily *and* you may feel the sensations especially strongly.

Another interoceptive cue that is often misinterpreted is the response you may have when you feel sensations in your genital area that you associate with sexual arousal, but it's happening at an unwanted or inappropriate time. This may occur because you are hypervigilant about such sensations and question their meaning, or you experience sexual arousal at an unwanted time. The reality is that genital responses are automatic and do not always indicate sexual desire. *Arousal non-concordance*—when your mind is saying no and your genitals are saying yes—is a common human experience. If your OCD is triggered by taboo content, you may also misinterpret other anxiety arousal as sexual arousal because you are monitoring your response to your triggers.

It's also true that the hyperawareness of autonomic functions such as breathing, blinking, swallowing, and heart rate that OCD predisposes you to can itself become part of the OCD maintenance cycle. That is, if you often notice sensations associated with anxiety, then the sensations themselves, and the anxiety they both signify and create, become a focus of your attention. A common obsession may be *Will I ever stop focusing on my hyperawareness?* This less common presentation of OCD varies from person to person. If you have this form of OCD, you may think you are being robbed of fully enjoying your life experiences because you are hyperaware of a bodily function.

As we discussed in the previous chapters, when an internal experience bothers you, you naturally want to suppress or get rid of it. Yet engaging with internal experiences you find problematic often magnifies the experience rather than getting rid of it. And really dealing with the experience in question requires dropping the struggle, counterintuitive as that may seem. It requires letting the anxiety and your hyperawareness of it be there long enough for you to realize that it *will* pass on its own and that you *can* in fact handle it.

Now that you have an understanding of what happens in your body when you have false alarms, let's look at how this appears in daily life.

How This Rule Affects Your Life

Often, a sensation that accompanies a thought can feel so real and be mistakenly interpreted as "proof" that the obsession is true. Let's look at some examples:

- After encountering a mysterious substance on the ground, Angela feels dizzy as she thinks *That substance is toxic and making me sick*. She showers, washes everything she wore, and asks for reassurance.

- Jonathon has a headache, feels hot, and can tell his heart is beating faster after noticing his frustration with thinking about thinking. He fears he will not perform tasks to his satisfaction, and he fears that he may suffer brain damage from overthinking.

- While feeling nauseous, Shawn thinks *I didn't wash my hands enough after changing my baby's diaper*. Shawn responds by washing his hands for an hour.

- After noticing a playful child, Courtney feels a tingling in her genitals while feeling out of breath, which she associates with sexual arousal, and thinks *I'm a pedophile*. She responds by avoiding children and trying to "figure out" whether she's dangerous.

- While cutting vegetables, Ryan has a "rush" through his body and feels shaky as he has an intrusive thoughts about stabbing his beloved dog, who is waiting for scraps. He responds by leaving the dog outside and moving the knives out of reach.

In these examples, the intolerable sensations and the interpretations further reinforce the validity of the obsession. Much like thoughts, interoceptive cues can be misinterpreted as an important signal rather than the noise that they are.

Regardless of your particular OCD theme, you may associate your thoughts, feelings, and physical sensations as dangerous, which leads you into your OCD maintenance cycle. Chad, who has obsessions about his relationship, describes it in this way:

When I look at my wife, I sometimes don't feel attracted to her. Sometimes I look at other women when I'm out and think they are attractive. When that happens, I have a surge of panic—I feel hot, I can feel my heart beating out of my chest, and I start hyperventilating. I feel like my stomach is turning somersaults when this happens. I can't stop thinking about whether I married the right woman. Am I settling for second best, or even worse? I can't get it out of my mind, so I avoid being close to her or going out with her much. I hate the way my anxiety feels, and I don't want to constantly be on alert for it, or for noticing other women when we're out. We get into exhausting discussions dissecting our relationship, and she reassures me that it's normal to find other women attractive. But it can't possibly be normal to feel this way. The more I try to figure this out once and for all, the more confused I am.

We see that Chad is feeling a range of sensations associated with his anxiety, which are exacerbating the stress of his OCD. He's extremely aware of his anxiety and the physical sensations associated with it, to the degree that avoiding the anxiety is becoming a primary driver for his behavior. He's also interpreting his sensations as adding validity to his triggering thoughts (*it can't possibly be normal to feel this way*). Now let's take a look at what following this rule makes daily life like for you.

Exercise: How Does Following the *Anxiety Means Danger Rule* Affect Your Life?

What physiological sensations do you notice when you are anxious? Do you avoid triggers that you associate with physical sensations? How do your sensations fit in with your OCD cycle? Write your obsessions, compulsions, and any avoidant behaviors you engage in.

How does following this rule impact your daily activities and doing what matters? Do you avoid associated triggers?

Picture your life without following this rule. What would you do differently? And is there a way you could do those things even now, whether anxiety's there or not?

Now let's look at skills that will help you to break this rule.

Breaking Free

To break free of this rule, you'll be changing your relationship with your sensations. Rather than interpreting sensation as dangerous and validating the thoughts that accompany them, you can learn to allow them to exist and to observe how they come and go, even as you pursue the actions that speak to what you truly value, rather than what your OCD "wants" you to do.

Using Body Awareness to Your Advantage

I'll start with a personal example: In yoga class several years ago, we were in a pose called Tadasana. When doing the pose correctly, you stand tall with shoulders back and sternum lifted. We stayed in the pose for what seemed to be ten minutes while our teacher gave us detailed instructions to enhance the pose. Breathing comes very freely in this stance, and the posture feels powerful. Outside of class, I began observing my own posture and that of others. I noticed that often, anxiety and distress is written in our very body language. Clients would hunch over, for instance, as though bracing against the stress of whatever they were dealing with.

Taking a protective stance to avoid your stress may seem like the right approach, but it may limit any belief that you can feel more powerful to face your fears. Let's explore what happens to your posture when you are anxious—and how you can change it to better allow sensations to come and go.

Exercise: Show Me with Your Body

(adapted from Steven Hayes)

Bring into your mind a disturbing OCD thought that you have found yourself struggling with. Now imagine you are a sculptor who can shape your body so that anyone looking at it would understand what it is like for you to deal with this OCD struggle. Either imagine or physically put your body in the posture that shows you when you are most entrenched in your OCD cycle. What do you notice? Stay with your internal experience as you curiously observe your thoughts, feelings, and sensations while in this posture. Notice what it feels like from inside of it. Mentally take a snapshot, then return to your normal posture and take a moment's break.

Now bring into your mind the same disturbing OCD thought that you are struggling with. Either imagine or physically put your body into the posture that shows you when you are open to experiencing your disturbing thought without fighting it. What do you notice? Stay with your internal experience as you curiously observe your thoughts, feelings, and sensations while in this posture. Notice what it feels like from inside of it. Mentally take a snapshot, then return to your normal posture.

What did you notice about how your body responds to each posture? How would you describe the difference between these two postures?

While imagining or in the first posture, did you notice your knuckles turning pale, your teeth grinding, or your jaw clenching? Did your breathing change, such as holding your breath or shallow breathing? These are common signs of internally fighting with your obsessions.

Adjusting your posture may help you to feel stronger as you face your fears. Your mindfulness practices will help you become more aware of how your posture changes as your emotional state changes. When you do ERP, check your posture and engage in your task with a powerful stance. Depending on the task you will do for your ERP, the following may be literal or figurative, but here are some steps to follow: Stand tall, feeling the soles of your feet on the ground. Lift your sternum, move your shoulders back, and step in the direction that matters to you. With practice, you might find you're better able to slow down and check your stance when you're in the midst of a compulsion that you want to stop, opening space for you to behave differently than you otherwise would.

Another tool to change your relationship with anxiety-related sensations—*interoceptive exposure*—will deepen your progress with ERP.

Inviting Uncomfortable Sensations to Be There

Interoceptive exposure is a series of exercises designed to re-create sensations in your body that are commonly associated with threat, so you can purposely activate beliefs you may have about the importance and meaning of anxious arousal, then address them. Interoceptive exposure will help you learn to tolerate the distress associated with your sensations and teach your brain that these sensations aren't dangerous, but innocuous. These exercises can help you practice allowing sensations and observing how their intensity rises and falls.

When you automatically interpret interoceptive cues as dangerous, you are overestimating how threatening a sensation or obsession is. And every time you respond to fear with compulsions and avoidance, you induce more fear. With interoceptive exposure, you'll engage in curiosity experiments to change your relationship with your anxiety.

Let's take a look at Chad's experience with interoceptive exposure.

Chad's Story

When Chad is triggered by the thought that he may not be attracted to his wife and notices attractions to other women while out in public, he interprets his accompanying sensations as a confirmation that his thoughts about his wife are valid. Chad's interoceptive exposure practice will focus on the sensations he experiences when he is triggered: hyperventilation, rapid heart rate, feeling hot, and a sensation of butterflies in his stomach.

First, Chad will come up with a list of ways he can trigger these sensations on purpose. For each task he comes up with, he'll rate the overall anxiety level he anticipates feeling, using 10 to represent the highest possible distress and 0 as no distress at all. He will rate the level of intensity of the sensations in the same way—10 representing highest imagined intensity, and 0 no intensity at all. He'll also rate how similar the exercise is to his actual experience when triggered, using a percentage from 0 to 100 that represents how similar the sensations are.

Once he has his list and ratings, he'll sort the exercises by how closely they're related to his experience of anxiety. Finally, he'll predict what he expects to happen while he completes the exercises, to complement the anxiety and intensity levels he's projected. After he's done each task, he'll record what he actually experienced during these exposure tasks.

Chad chooses the following interoceptive exposure exercises to complete, one right after the other:

- Wearing a turtleneck, eat something and then breathe in rapid pants for one minute.

- For one minute each, run up and down the stairs, then spin in a swivel chair, and then do jumping jacks.

- Take his pulse to feel the sensation of his heart beating.

- Swivel his head side to side for one minute.

- Breathe through a straw with fast shallow breaths for five seconds longer than he thinks he can.

- Hold a wall pushup at the halfway point for thirty seconds.

He decides he'll repeat this series of interoceptive exposure activities three times, twice a day. With curiosity, he will observe his response to the rise and fall of intense sensations in his body. Once he completes the exercises, he can record his responses and reflect on what he learned from the experience. It is important for him to articulate whether his predicted expectations matched his actual experience. In addition to this daily curiosity experiment, Chad can gradually experiment with changing the ordering of the tasks and seeing what happens. To deepen his learning, he will practice doing the interoceptive exposure both alone and in combination with other exposures.

Chad is choosing to work aggressively on his ERP; you are in charge of the pace at which you work. You can move much more gradually if you wish.

To enhance learning, Chad will combine his interoceptive tasks while thinking *Maybe my experience in my relationship is only second best or even worse.* While doing his interoceptive exposure, he can either think the triggering thought or listen to it on a recording device set to repeat. In this way, Chad can learn that the thoughts and sensations that he has been avoiding are simply noise.

Now let's take a look at the steps you'll take to personalize your own interoceptive exposure exercises. Some people with anxiety sensitivity also have a medical condition that makes it difficult to determine whether they are experiencing body noise due to anxiety or a signal that needs attention. This is another reason to team up with your physician for clearance and work on these exercises with a therapist who specializes in ERP for anxiety disorders and OCD.

As with all the ERP that you do, approach these exercises with curiosity and observe what you experience moment to moment.

Exercise: Experiencing Uncomfortable Sensations (part 1)

First, identify exercises that re-create the sensations that trigger your anxiety. To do this, experiment with several tasks and record your overall anxiety level (0 to 10) and whether the exercise produced sensations similar to the ones that you interpret as threatening (0 to 100 percent). You'll need a timer and either your journal or a form (available at http://www.newharbinger.com/51024) to record your responses. Make adjustments based on your fitness level and medical conditions.

For fear of feeling out of breath:

- Hyperventilate for sixty seconds by taking rapid deep breaths.

- Watch the second hand on a clock while pinching your nose closed and holding your breath for as long as you can. Stay with it for a few seconds past what you think you can do.

- While pinching your nose closed, breathe through a cocktail straw with fast, shallow breaths. Again, stay with it for a few seconds past what you think you can do.

- To increase your heart rate, run in place, do jumping jacks, or run up and down stairs for two minutes.

For the next set of tasks, for fears of dizziness and lightheadedness, you'll need plenty of space and no tripping hazards. You can place a chair nearby to balance yourself if needed when you stop the exercise. It's best to start with a swivel chair so you can practice experiencing lightheadedness and dizziness while seated. Once you have practiced this, then you can move to walking in small circles and spinning. When performing any tasks that make you dizzy or lightheaded, be aware that when you stop, you may feel off balance. If you do, pause and look at a spot on the wall until the feeling passes.

- Swivel your head from side to side by looking to the left, then the right at a pace of one rotation per second for one minute.

- In a sitting position, bend over and place your head between your knees. Hold this position for about thirty seconds. Then quickly straighten up to a sitting position. Repeat.

- Sit in a swivel chair and spin the chair while looking straight ahead for sixty seconds.

- Walk in small (beach ball size) circles while looking straight in front of you for sixty seconds. Be aware that when you stop you may feel off balance.

- While sitting tall with your eyes closed, gently move your chin down toward your chest and roll your head in a circle.

For fears of feeling shaky or feeling tense:

- Drink a highly caffeinated beverage.

- Hold a plank or pushup position until you feel shaky.

- Hold a pushup position halfway down or do pushups until you feel shaky.

- Do a squat with your back against the wall and hold this position until you feel shaky.

- Hold light weights with your arms extended in front of you until you feel shaky.

- In a seated position, raise one knee straight up so that your foot is a few inches from the floor and the back of your thigh is lifted slightly off the chair seat. Either hold the position or slowly move your knee up and down.

- In a seated position, tense your body and hold for one minute. If you have a particular body area where you experience tingling, shakiness, or numbness, target that area and bring tension to it for one minute.

Hold each task for several seconds past what you think you can do. The time period for each exercise depends on your fitness level and physiological health.

For fears related to your heart, do an exercise that increases your heart rate, such as running in place.

For fears of chest tightness, wear a tight band or belt around your chest and do some jumping jacks or run in place.

For feelings of nonreality or feeling detached, allow your focus to soften while doing the following tasks:

- Stare at your hand for two minutes.

- Stare at yourself in the mirror in a room with low light for two minutes.

- Stare at a spot on the wall for two to three minutes.

- Stare at an optical illusion, such as a spiral.

- Do an online search for videos of spiral optical illusions.

- Wear spiral swirly glasses that you can buy at a party store.

- Wear the spiral swirly glasses while you spin in a swivel chair.

For fears of stomach upset:

- Wear tight clothes around your belly.

- Eat a little too much and jump up and down.

- Tightly squeeze a firm pillow to your chest and belly and hold it for one minute.

For fear of choking or tightness in your throat, swallow quickly five times in a row.

For fear of feeling too hot, do the following tasks:

- Wear warm clothing while exercising.

- Eat a hot spicy food.

- Take a hot shower.

Exercise: Experiencing Uncomfortable Sensations (part 2)

The next step is to take a look at your recorded responses to the exercises and prepare a list of tasks that closely re-create the ones that trigger your anxiety. You can use your journal or download a tracking form, the Interoceptive Exposure Tracking Log, at http://www.newharbinger.com/51024.

Make a list of the exercises and vary the order based on the level of intensity and distress that you feel with each exercise. For example, if hyperventilation was highly intense and created high distress for you, follow that exercise with a less-challenging one. If you have just been re-creating dizziness, don't run up and down stairs immediately afterward. If these exercises are highly activating, you may want to start with one or two and do those for several days before adding additional challenging ones. Don't be concerned about whether you have the exercises in the "right" order. Follow the above guidelines and order them as you wish. And this is essential: Complete the exposure tasks only if you are 100-percent all-in with experiencing whatever sensations and feelings show up.

Before completing the exercises, make sure you articulate what you predict will happen as a result of completing them. Now practice what is on your list. Take only enough of a break in between exercises to record your intensity and anxiety level. Move quickly down your list and do the sequence two to four times in a row.

After you complete your exercises, reflect on whether your experiences matched your prediction of what would happen. What did you learn?

Once you have practiced interoceptive exposure regularly and you are willing to make the ERP more challenging, experiment with reordering your tasks, and notice the difference. You can enhance your learning by adding a triggering thought during your tasks and doing these tasks where you are likely to be triggered.

If you are hyperaware of autonomic functions in your body, such as breathing, swallowing, blinking, or thinking, then you'll work on doing a

180-degree pivot and allow the awareness with openness without trying to make it go away. You can learn to coexist with the automatic body functions that your mind is hyperfocused on. An ERP task that can be helpful is to practice purposely attending to the sensation you are hyper-aware of. For example, Jennifer feared that her experiences would be partially ruined because of her hyperawareness of swallowing. So she set a timer fifteen times a day to purposely practice bringing her awareness to her swallowing. She started out by attending to the sensation for one minute at a time, building up to attending to it for five minutes. As she attended to the sensation, she observed her experience and practiced allowing it to coexist in her mind. Jennifer has feared feeling awkward and embarrassed with her friends because they might notice her hyper-awareness of swallowing or that she appears distracted and not completely focused on them during activities. It is crucial that she include social activities such as eating meals with her friends in her ERP menu.

Points to Remember

Your body responds to the emotions you feel when you are anxious. You may feel sensations associated with your threat system. Interoceptive cues are your sensations from inside your body; you can misinterpret these as being dangerous or adding validity to your triggering thoughts, because they seem so real. And as long as you avoid or perform compulsions to eliminate your discomfort, you'll be more sensitive and fearful of the sensations in your body. You can learn to effectively coexist with uncomfortable sensations and live life fully.

In this chapter, you have learned ways to change your relationship with your uncomfortable sensations and accompanying thoughts. You have learned that you can be mindful of your posture toward your experiences—both figuratively and literally. Adjusting your posture may help you feel more confident in yourself to be all-in with ERP and more actively participate in life.

You have learned that interoceptive exposure is a powerful tool that you can combine with other exposures. You are developing an effective and varied repertoire of skills you can use to change your relationship with your obsessions and break the rules of your OCD.

In the chapters ahead, you will widen your repertoire still further with new skills to help you live life flexibly and free from the rules of OCD.

CHAPTER 8

Responsibility Has Limits

In this chapter, we will address how to break the OCD rule *You alone are responsible if you fail to prevent harm.* Inflating your level of responsibility to prevent negative outcomes is a common tendency associated with OCD. In response to this belief—that you alone are responsible if harms that you could conceivably have prevented occur—you may engage in checking and reassurance compulsions to prevent harm to yourself or others, which then strengthens your belief that it was your compulsions that prevented the bad thing from happening.

Examining when you are taking too much responsibility for an outcome, taking steps to reduce rituals with ERP, and navigating your feelings of guilt will help you break this rule.

What Drives the *Responsibility to Prevent Harm* Rule

Responsibility is a desirable attribute that people frequently notice in others. When colleagues or loved ones appreciate and compliment this quality in you, it is reinforcing. Yet it's possible to take on *too much* responsibility—to believe you hold the power to cause or prevent negative outcomes (Taylor 2002). Again, overestimation of one's personal responsibility is a core feature of OCD. You may routinely make decisions based on an

inflated sense of responsibility that contributes to your OCD maintenance cycle.

The negative outcomes that result from this distorted sense of your
own responsibility can vary—from magical beliefs, such as *If I do something at a bad luck time, something bad will happen and it will be my fault*, to
realistic fears such as worrying that you forgot to lock a door and so have
put yourself, your loved ones, your pets, or your belongings in danger from
intruders, leading you to obsessive checking and rumination. The greater
the responsibility you feel, the more checking you may engage in
(Bouchard, Rhéaume, and Ladouceur 1999), such as checking door locks
or making sure you really did send an important email. And checking
leads you to increased doubts and repetition and undermines your confidence in your memory.

A tendency to overestimate responsibility for situations is often
closely related to a tendency to overestimate the possibility of harm from
a situation. It's common to believe you are solely responsible for preventing harm. Your mind tells you that if you don't control the outcome of
situations, everything that might happen will be your fault. And there's
endless potential for your mind to tell you that you're responsible for preventing harm. This preoccupation keeps you vigilantly looking for potential harm that could come to others, and you see yourself as responsible
for preventing it. It also keeps you engaged in mental time travel: living in
a future of what-if scenarios rather than in the present moment.

You may try to control events that are uncontrollable by using avoidance, as well as rituals to exert control over a situation you believe is
potentially dangerous. In your mind, you may exaggerate your power over
events and other people. And when you try to overcontrol events, you
may miss information that could help you assess the situation more realistically. You may engage in polarized thinking, viewing two opposite
extremes with no middle ground. Examples of polarized thinking include
beliefs that

- Not performing a compulsion means you actually *want* a terrible
  event to happen.

- Failing to prevent harm is equal to causing harm.

- Not doing a compulsion to erase the negative thought means you want the thought to be true.

With inflated responsibility and risk of harm, you may recognize that what your mind is telling you is a low-probability event, but you still find the risk completely unacceptable. You create a double standard for responsibilities and perfectionism, holding yourself to a higher standard than others. You may even experience a sense of specialness, thinking you need to be held to a higher standard to survive (McGrath 2006).

No matter what you are obsessing about, you believe that if you take certain actions, you can control the outcome—which reinforces your OCD cycle. When you avoid activities that you associate with disaster or engage in compulsions such as checking, and the bad thing doesn't happen, you are reinforcing your belief that avoidance or other compulsions are effective strategies.

At the heart of this rule, which may have you taking too much personal responsibility for situations, are feelings of anxiety and guilt. People with OCD often perceive guilt as a threat; the feeling of guilt from perceiving that you are responsible when something goes wrong, or feeling that if you don't take responsibility you are a bad person, is extremely uncomfortable. Feelings of guilt stem from thoughts of responsibility and blame. You may blame yourself for things that are completely out of your control. You may also find feelings of guilt frightening and unbearable, so you avoid triggers and perform compulsions.

Guilt may also come from the way you value being of service, being helpful, and always being there for others. In this way, OCD can hijack your values so that your desire to be of service becomes intense fear of not doing enough for others—not being a constantly generous, caring, helpful, empathetic, and trustworthy person. Do you find that others ask you to take on responsibilities to help? You may feel a sense of purpose and have positive feelings about being needed; you may also find yourself overloaded with tasks and feeling resentful. Your values may also be hijacked by your desire to protect others. This can "require" you to take extreme safety measures, and people you care about may find your behavior overly controlling—creating friction instead of closer relationships.

Now that you have an understanding of what drives this rule, let's look at how it may affect your life.

How This Rule Affects Your Life

Let's look at some examples of how the rule *You alone are responsible if you fail to prevent harm* operates in people's lives.

- Krista worries that if she doesn't touch certain things four times, something bad will happen to her family.

- While driving, Abu hits a bump in the road and obsesses that he hit a pedestrian. He repeatedly drives by the street to check, and he searches the news online.

- After preparing a nice meal for guests, Sean fears the meat wasn't defrosted right and everyone will get sick. He calls the store where he bought the meat to get reassurance and engages in excessive online searching.

- Leslie removes sticks, rocks, and other items from the sidewalk to prevent someone from tripping.

- Terry checks locks and appliances before leaving home and at bedtime. She is on probation at work for tardiness and is exhausted from sleep deprivation because of the excessive time it takes to check.

- Lance prays excessively out of fear that he might be responsible for a tragedy that could happen in future years.

- Ahmed fears being responsible for spreading germs that will cause others to be ill and washes his hands excessively.

- Tim mentally reviews past situations that had negative outcomes to determine whether he was responsible for those outcomes.

- Alissa often says "I'm sorry" excessively.

- Zach fears that he is responsible for the damage associated with hurricane Harvey.

There are various signs that could indicate you are following this rule by avoiding activities that you may associate with disaster, such as using appliances, saying bad luck numbers or words, driving, and making decisions. You may find yourself trying too hard on tasks and in your relationships. Taking on responsibility to prevent harm is time consuming, frightening, and exhausting. Feeling guilty can motivate you to do compulsions and feel badly about yourself.

Exercise: The *You Alone Are Responsible* Rule

Reflect on how you follow the rule *You alone are responsible if you fail to prevent harm* by identifying specific thoughts, compulsions, and avoidant behavior that you engage in. How does following this rule affect your quality of life and constrain you from pursuing things that matter to you?

Now that you know the signs indicating that you follow this rule, we'll address how you can break it.

Breaking Free

In addition to the skills you have learned in other chapters to target your obsessions related to inflated responsibility and risks, in this section you'll learn how to develop healthy responsibility and gradually eliminate rituals, explore how guilt plays a role in your behavior, and design exposures that target your inflated sense of responsibility and guilt.

Developing Healthy Responsibility

To break this rule, you must accept that risks are part of life, and your responsibility has limits. No matter how much responsibility you take on to prevent harm, there is no such thing as 100-percent safety. Chances are you hold yourself to a higher standard than others when your mind sees the potential for harm. It is crucial that you give up your double standard and treat yourself the way you would treat others. For example, when Leslie, who takes it upon herself to move sticks or rocks out of the way on the sidewalk to keep others from tripping, is asked whether she expects everyone else to do this, she responds with a quick "Of course not!" And it's clearly unreasonable to expect that she alone is responsible for whether anyone trips over a random rock or stick in the sidewalk. It's her OCD telling her that she has the power to prevent negative outcomes and that if she doesn't, she's responsible.

How can you give up your double standards?

Exercise: Giving Up Your Double Standard

Make a list of responsibilities that you take on to prevent negative outcomes.

Identify family, friends, or role models whom you believe are responsible citizens. If they encountered similar situations in which you perform compulsions driven by inflated responsibility, would you expect them to perform the same compulsions? If there was a bad outcome, would you blame them?

When comparing your standards to those of other responsible people, do you find that you hold yourself to a different standard of responsibility in order to prevent negative outcomes? Chances are you do.

To break this rule, consider what you need to change in order to live by the same standard that any reasonable person would strive to meet. Now make a list of what you would do differently to live by the same standards you have for others. You'll use this information to design your ERP practices.

To illustrate the skills you can use to break this rule, let's look at an example. Keep in mind that regardless of what OCD symptoms you experience, you'll follow the same steps discussed in previous chapters to make gradual changes while modifying your rituals. Also, if you have scrupulous obsessions, the faith/morality statement in this story will be particularly useful to you.

Tanisha's Story

Tanisha obsesses about the safety of her family and holds herself responsible for keeping them safe with her compulsions. She performs a prayer ritual twice a day in which she says a unique prayer for each of her eleven family members. If she doesn't say each prayer perfectly, she believes she is offending God and will be responsible for causing harm to her family in the future. Each family member's prayer requires different words that she must state exactly right. The entire ritual is extremely time consuming and exhausting.

For Tanisha to prepare for ERP, she will work to differentiate between her religious beliefs and OCD beliefs (Pollard 2004) and prepare a faith/morality statement, to begin setting her faith apart from her OCD. Two aspects of Tanisha's religion that are particularly relevant to her OCD are the nature of God and the purpose of prayer. In her statement, she writes "God is loving and forgives me for my sins without punishing me. Prayer is talking with God and includes thanking him and asking for guidance, forgiveness, and protection. God is wise and can determine my intent, so it isn't necessary to say my prayers exactly right. God knows my heart."

The next step is for Tanisha to write what her OCD has to say about the nature of God and prayer. She writes, "God will punish me by allowing terrible things to happen to my family if I don't pray exactly right."

She then considers the two statements. She determines that she feels distant from God when she engages in the kind of ritualized prayer that stems from her OCD, and she feels more connected when she thinks about the belief based on her religion.

For Tanisha to break this rule, she will gradually eliminate the steps in her prayer ritual and will not ask others for the reassurance that has been a big part of her ritual. She will use her faith statement, rather than her OCD, as a guide to live by. She often feels guilty about the possibility that something bad could happen to her family because she didn't pray according to the OCD rules. As she thinks about how she can pray in a way that's consistent with her religious beliefs, she decides that it's reasonable to pray for everyone at once, rather than requiring a unique prayer for each person. The exception would be if someone is ill, traveling, or needs extra support. In this case, she wants to limit her prayer for this person to one sentence that addresses the issue.

Next, Tanisha describes the "rules" of the ritual she wants to eliminate. She relies on some typical considerations for anyone working to understand and eliminate a ritual, regardless of what obsession is driving it.

Does the ritual need to be completed in a particular order? If so, write down the order of each step.

Is there a specific location or position that your body must be in as you complete the ritual?

Are there "props" required?

Do any behaviors have to be repeated?

Are there special numbers, words, or gestures?

Do you involve others in your ritual?

As she answers these questions, Tanisha realizes that she recites all her prayers in the same basic sequence:

Dear heavenly Father,

I would like to pray for [the family member], who I love so much

Pray for safety

Pray that certain positive things will occur

Please, please, please hear my prayer

I'm grateful to you

Thanks for allowing me to have my family

Amen, amen, amen

She also notes that she repeats each prayer three times for each family member, unless she feels she hasn't said it exactly right. In that case, all the prayers previously completed are invalidated, so she has to start over. As she's praying, she must kneel toward a wall displaying a picture of Jesus and hold her Bible.

Another compulsive behavior Tanisha engages in is sending each family member a morning greeting to get reassurance that they are okay. At first glance, this appears to be thoughtful, values-based behavior because she loves her family. But she is actually sending those family greetings to get relief from her obsession and anxiety. If she doesn't get a response, she gets extremely anxious and seeks out confirmation that they are safe.

To accomplish eliminating rituals, you will need to break the rules of the ritual, taking whatever steps you choose. It's unrealistic to expect to immediately eliminate a ritual you are struggling with. I'm sure you have already thought of that, or been told to "just stop ritualizing." But if it were that easy, you would have already done it. Eliminating a ritual is always challenging. For Tanisha, it raises a fear that this could jeopardize someone's life.

But if she works one step at a time, it'll be easier to loosen the grip her obsessions and rituals have on her. Tanisha will start with leaving out the word "heavenly" and eliminating the second line of each prayer ("Dear heavenly father, I would like to pray for my mom, who I love so much"). She will make the assumption that God knows that she loves her mother. Her prayer will start with "Dear father, I pray for my mom's safety," followed by the rest of her ritual. In her exposure menu, she plans to further break the rules of her ritual as follows:

- Leaving out the phrase "I'm grateful to you"

- Facing a different direction from the picture of Jesus

- Keeping the Bible on a table

- Not sending greetings to family members each morning

- Saying amen once at the end of her prayers for each family member

- Rather than saying "Dear God" as she prays for each family member, saying it once at the beginning of her prayer time

- Limiting the word "please" to one time

- Saying amen once at the end of her prayers for each family member

With these many small steps, she can gradually eliminate the prayer ritual and shift her prayers to a more general, spiritual format. Using her mindfulness skills, Tanisha stays in the moment as she says her prayers and notices her internal experience as she prays. In time, Tanisha will notice the difference between what it feels like to do a spiritual prayer and an OCD ritualized prayer. She allows her internal experience to come and go. And in time, noticing her exhaustion and the inconvenience of ritualizing compared to the peaceful experience of a spiritual prayer, she feels more motivation to eliminate her ritual.

Exercise: Ending a Ritual

Think of a ritual that you would like to eliminate, and write the steps, using the considerations just mentioned. Create an exposure menu with ideas of how you'll gradually eliminate steps of your ritual.

Tanisha's Story: Experiencing Guilt

Tanisha feels guilty if anyone in her family encounters an unexpected challenge in their day. Although she is aware that the shit hits the fan sometimes in everyone's life, when it comes to her family, she believes she is more responsible for their suffering because it means she didn't do her rituals correctly enough. She apologizes profusely, even for mishaps that aren't her fault, and tries to make up for it by doing something special for the "victim." This may include cooking their favorite meal or repeatedly asking them what she can do for them. Unexpected events often exacerbate her prayer rituals and reassurance seeking. She also fears that if she doesn't do something to make up for mishaps her family experiences in daily life, she would not be able to cope with the guilt she'd feel. Guilt influences her decisions in daily life and blocks her from taking care of herself by getting proper sleep, nutrition, and relaxation. Her mind tells her that she is not worthy of attending to her own needs.

It is important for Tanisha to differentiate when guilt is the motivator for her behavior, and to let go of her perception of her internal experience of guilt as intolerable. To help her break this rule about being overly responsible for others' well-being, she needs to practice allowing guilt to be present and staying with it to see what happens. She makes a list of how she avoids feeling guilty, which includes getting stuck in her prayer rituals, reassurance seeking, excessive apologizing, and doing kind things for her family when they have a bad day.

Tanisha values being a kind and generous person. It is important for her to determine whether actions that feel like expressions of kind, generous behavior are leading her to a healthy life or moving her in an unhealthy direction that robs her of the life she wants. If your kind, generous behavior is motivated by guilt, what are the consequences? By keeping up with her ERP and being mindful of and willing to accept what arises when she does, Tanisha will learn that she can be the kind, generous person that she is and take care of herself and tolerate the feelings of guilt that might arise when she doesn't perform her OCD compulsions.

If you suspect you struggle with guilt, ask yourself *Is my behavior motivated by guilt or the values I hold?* Just like Tanisha, you may find that your values get hijacked by your OCD, making the task of identifying your motivation more challenging.

Tanisha thought through the consequences of her compulsions to answer this question for herself. She recruited her family to encourage her to take care of herself, and to express gentle but explicit discomfort when she engages in kind behaviors to make up for their bad days, with the goal of reinforcing for her that these are behaviors driven by guilt, and she doesn't need to do them. She also made a guilt exposure menu and used values-based exposure so she could allow herself to experience her reaction to guilt. And she decided to work on not apologizing and, on a day when a family member has a mishap, doing a nurturing activity for herself rather than engaging in compulsions.

Exercise: Guilt Exposure Menu

When does guilt show up in your life and what is your typical response? How does it interfere with your living the life you want? Make a guilt exposure menu and set some SMART goals and complete values-based ERP.

Points to Remember

Overestimation of responsibility is usually closely related to overestimating risks of a bad outcome. To overcome it, it's crucial to accept that you can't eliminate all risks from life. When you give up your double standard in favor of living by the same standard you expect from others, you may feel guilt, as well as relief—and ERP that evokes feelings of guilt can be instrumental in breaking this rule.

In the next chapter, you will learn skills that will help you color outside the lines to break the rule that states *Everything must be just right*. You're continuing to increase your repertoire of skills to break the rules of OCD.

CHAPTER 9

Color Outside the Lines

This chapter will help you learn to break a rule driven by perfectionism: *Everything must be just right*. Perfectionism can play a role in the maintenance of your OCD. It can contribute to avoidance of tasks and is central in OCD themes involving symmetry, order, slowness, scrupulosity, feeling incomplete, and a sense of "it's not just right." This chapter aims to help you examine where perfectionism pays off for you and where it serves as a barrier to living the life you want. Rather than viewing imperfection as a catastrophe that means something terrible, you can strive for excellence and perform the best that you can. To succeed with whatever you want to accomplish, it's important to learn to flexibly respond to your daily life and its unexpected triggers, mistakes, and mishaps. You can learn to change unhelpful perfectionistic behaviors as you use your values as a guide.

What Drives the *Everything Must Be Just Right* Rule

A working group of experts studying obsessive-compulsive thinking patterns defined perfectionism as "the tendency to believe there is a perfect solution to every problem, that doing something perfectly is not only possible, but also necessary, and that even minor mistakes will have serious consequences" (Obsessive Compulsive Cognitions Working Group 1997, 678). Generally, perfectionism is striving for flawlessness, and when taken to the extreme, it affects everything in your life (Flett and Hewitt 2002). Perfectionism is an important cognitive factor in OCD (Taylor 2002).

That said, perfectionism is multidimensional, so its impact varies considerably from person to person. But you can divide the many dimensions into two broad categories: maladaptive evaluation concerns and positive achievement striving (Frost et al. 1993). Maladaptive evaluation concerns that create anxiety include concern over mistakes, doubts about actions you might take, criticism and high standards set by parents, and self-imposed perfectionistic standards. Positive striving involves having high standards for yourself and others, neatness, and organization. You and others may value your positive striving and your ability to critically evaluate your efforts to improve.

Perfectionism contributes to a rigid style of all-or-nothing thinking in which you worry that minor errors may create catastrophic consequences. Consequences you may fear include other people thinking of you as a complete failure, or a sense you are not "good enough" as a person. When you have a specific standard in mind, you may doubt your ability to meet this standard, so you procrastinate on beginning an important task. When you do begin, rather than acting with curiosity and openness to whatever might arise, you focus on preventing failure. Once you begin a task, you may doubt whether you have performed it "right," which keeps you focused on the threat of not meeting your expectation rather than the fulfillment that can come when you're performing an action because you're passionate about it or just curious about the result. Perfectionism also stifles your creativity because you are narrowly focused on your fear of imperfection.

How This Rule Affects Your Life

There's no getting around it: Life is messy. No matter how hard you try to control things, you'll still encounter this reality. Routine daily events can bring unpredictable hassles with them, and everyone will experience such hassles from time to time. You may find that you try to control things in your life to feel safe and certain that you are free from harsh criticism by others as well as yourself. Compulsions can be a way to avoid the anxiety of recognizing that imperfections can and do occur in everyday life (Frost and DiBartolo 2002).

Perfectionism can also be a barrier to engaging in and implementing treatment for your OCD. You may have expectations that as you do ERP, you'll find fast relief from the disorder, and that with each ERP practice you'll experience the same amount of success. But realistically, you can expect progress to feel like several steps forward, a step or two backward, and then a step forward again.

Similarly, you may have great intentions to follow your ERP plans perfectly throughout your day, every day, but you'll likely find that life gets in the way, and your practice might be harder sometimes. Inevitably, some days of practice will be easier and some will be harder. Also, none of us function the same way every single day. You might be moving through triggers quite easily and feel proud of yourself, only to find that an unexpected event sets you back. Progress isn't a linear downward slope of decreasing anxiety. It appears more like a sawtooth—expect that the slope may go down, plateau a bit, and go down a bit, spike up a bit, and then go down again. The true measure of your success with ERP will be that you are engaging in life, doing what matters to you even while you are anxious.

A subtype of OCD that is associated with perfectionism is symmetry, order, and arranging (SOA), and is driven by "not just right" experiences (NJRE), imperfection, and incompletion (Clark 2020). In this subtype, instead of fear of harm triggering compulsions, a sensory-based state—a bodily sense of discomfort that your brain registers as a sign that something is not just right—is the motivator. The sensory experience may be an external trigger, such as visual perception of asymmetry, or something internal, like a sensation of discomfort. Incompleteness is a sense that something isn't finished. Compulsions you might engage in because of this type of OCD could involve ordering, repeating, and arranging to achieve order, symmetry, and completeness. Fear of uncomfortable internal NJREs lasting forever and leading to a loss of control if you don't do your compulsions contribute to the OCD maintenance cycle.

In summary, perfectionism can be driven by avoiding anything that triggers internal discomfort—experiencing fear, shame, guilt, or a sensory experience of not feeling "just right." And it often leads to time-consuming compulsions, meticulous checking, and performing tasks painfully slowly to do things "just right."

- Tia spends three hours in the bathroom meticulously applying her makeup and styling her hair to look exactly perfect.

- Gabriel washes objects so his belongings are in pristine condition.

- Alexa takes excessive time getting out of a chair. She must feel just right before fully standing up.

- Candace has to have things look symmetrical and exact.

- When Mike touches something with the left side of his body, he doesn't feel right until he touches that thing with the right side.

- Debbie is devoted to following her religious beliefs to an unrealistic standard to avoid going to hell.

- Seth turns light switches on and off until it feels just right. He can't really explain that feeling; he knows when it's okay to stop flipping them on and off. He adds, "I don't think I can ever live with the not-just-right feeling."

- Tate avoids completion of tasks because they need to be perfect. He feels anxious when he must do things, because he always doubts whether the task is completed correctly.

- Zoe is indecisive and feels paralyzed by her need to choose the most perfect option. She spends excessive amounts of time researching decisions she has to make online to achieve certainty that she made the right choice.

- Anthony questions whether he is doing his ERP perfectly and whether he has the perfect therapist for him. His treatment is often derailed as he seeks out reassurance with online searches and spends time talking to new therapists about his treatment.

Exercise: The *Everything Must Be Just Right* Rule

Reflect on how you follow the rule *Everything must be just right* by identifying specific thoughts, compulsions, and avoidant behavior that you engage in.

Then consider how following this rule affects your quality of life and impacts carrying out behaviors that matter to you.

Now that you know what it looks like to follow the rule *Everything must be just right*, we'll address how to break it.

Breaking Free

Perfectionism involves learned behavioral patterns that can be helpful or unhelpful depending on the outcomes they create in your life (Kemp 2020). You and others may value your positive striving and your ability to critically evaluate your efforts in order to improve. If striving for perfection and being able to mentally step back and evaluate your efforts compassionately opens up meaningful experiences in your life, then you are experiencing helpful perfectionism.

Helpful perfectionism is perfectionism motivated by and in the service of things that you care about. When you experience it, although you may sometimes feel anxious about the outcome you are working toward, you can accept that your best effort is good enough no matter what happens. Ultimately, helpful perfectionism allows you to use your curiosity, creativity, and values to freely choose actions courageously, with no agenda besides giving your best effort. You accept any mistakes you might make as an opportunity to learn and improve.

In contrast, unhelpful perfectionism is driven by avoiding unpleasant internal experiences such as fear of failure. Behavior is motivated by a need to avoid mistakes and scrutiny. This tends to narrow your thinking and create rigid behavioral patterns as you are invested in a certain outcome that is not attainable or creates unpleasant consequences such as disappointment, isolation, distress, and exhaustion. Ultimately, unhelpful perfectionism moves you away from what matters to you and creates difficulties. Others may view the outcome you achieve as outstanding, but you can't feel good about your accomplishment because of what your perfectionism has cost you—and because the bar could always be set higher. And again, you view any mistakes as signs of failure and reasons to see yourself as ineffective.

Moving from unhelpful to helpful perfectionism will involve identifying where the disadvantages of your perfectionism outweigh the benefits, identifying where perfectionistic behaviors interfere with what is important to you, and creating cognitive and behavioral flexibility. You then can courageously employ a variety of strategies to break the cycle of perfectionism and pursue behaviors that earn you life outcomes you truly value.

To live a fulfilling life, based on what is important to you, it is important to discriminate between helpful and unhelpful perfectionism. A cost-benefit analysis will help you identify the advantages and disadvantages of your perfectionism. This can help you change behavioral patterns that aren't expanding your life in a meaningful way even though your intentions are good. You then can see the reality of your behavior rather than the story you tell yourself about why you need to maintain your perfectionism. This tool can help motivate you to experiment with alternatives that are more sustainable for living a healthy and fulfilling life.

Exercise: Cost-Benefit Analysis for Perfectionism

Divide a page of your journal into four quadrants by drawing a vertical line down the middle of the page and a horizontal line approximately halfway down the page (or download a form and a completed example from http://www. newharbinger.com/51024). In the upper left quadrant, write "Disadvantages of my perfectionism" and list them. For example, your perfectionism could be time consuming and exhausting, leaving you with little time to enjoy being with your family. Consider how your perfectionism impacts your relationships with your family, your social life, your performance or experience at work or school, your health, your spiritual life, the leisure activities you do or don't do, your experiences of your community, and your environment.

In the upper right quadrant write the heading "Advantages of my perfectionism" and list them. For example, you may receive positive feedback from others about your work. Or maybe your perfectionism has helped you achieve things in your life that are truly meaningful to you.

In the lower left quadrant, write the heading "Advantages of modifying perfectionism" and list them. For example, you may feel that modifying your unhelpful perfectionism at work will leave you with more energy and more time to enjoy your relationships.

In the lower right quadrant, write the heading "Disadvantages of modifying perfectionism" and list whatever you fear might happen if you change your perfectionist behaviors. For example, you may fear that you'll become lazy and settle for mediocre standards, leading to conflict with your coworkers.

As you review this exercise, write your responses to the following questions:

- How does your perfectionism work for you? Is it sustainable over time?

- Are there disadvantages to maintaining perfectionism that outweigh the advantages?

- Can you be the person you want to be while maintaining your perfectionism in its current form?

- What important values are you sacrificing by maintaining your perfectionism in its current form?

- Are there any changes you want to make that can help you transform from unhealthy to healthy perfectionism? This means transforming currently problematic perfectionism into a kind of perfectionism that serves your values and your quality of life and doesn't impede your progress toward these things.

Transforming your perfectionism will require some experimentation as you learn what works for you. Let's look at how Rebecca uses her cost-benefit analysis to help her identify behaviors she wants to change.

Rebecca's Story

Rebecca, a family practice physician who is passionate about how she cares for her patients, has high standards for tasks she completes. She values doing a great job and enjoys the feedback she gets from her patients and colleagues. But her high standards are driven by a fear of making mistakes. Rebecca says, "Writing emails is a nightmare, and if I get most of the way through the email and I don't like the way it sounds, I delete it and start over." She estimates that she spends at least triple the time and effort that her work colleagues do to complete simple tasks. Documenting her visits with her patients, reviewing reports, and completing forms is important to make sure she doesn't jeopardize any of her patient's health. She rechecks her work for accuracy as she documents so she makes good recommendations for the people she cares for.

We can all appreciate a physician, in particular, having high standards. But Rebecca finds that she's exhausted when she arrives home and is often cranky with her wife and children after a long day of work where she runs behind schedule and skips lunch. She promises her children that she will read with them but usually falls asleep before she can. She also feels guilty and sad about yelling at her family when they want time with her.

Rebecca lists these disadvantages of her perfectionism:

- *Feeling guilty about yelling at family*
- *Missing quality time with family*
- *Working to exhaustion*
- *Having difficulty sleeping*
- *Resenting how it robs me of my time*
- *Being hypercritical of myself*
- *Feeling terrified of making mistakes*

Turning to advantages, she writes:

- *Feeling satisfaction*
- *Reducing anxiety, knowing I checked my work carefully*
- *Earning praise from patients and coworkers*

As Rebecca reflects on her cost-benefit analysis, she is surprised by the costs of her perfectionism and saddened again by the toll it's taken on her family and health. She realizes this pattern is unsustainable for her health and family life. At the same time, she values being a good physician for her patients and knows it will be challenging to modify her behavior by checking less and lowering her standards. Her mind is mentally time traveling, with questions like What if I make a mistake? What if my patients get upset with me? What if my colleagues lose respect for me?

But in the end, Rebecca doesn't want to sacrifice her health and family to maintain her standards. To transform her unhelpful perfectionism, she will work on a variety of ERP practices focused on gradually letting go of her compulsive checking behaviors. As she learns from her experiences, she can gradually find the right balance so she is not sacrificing important values related to her roles as a physician, mother, and wife.

Rather than starting over on writing emails that she views as somehow "wrong," she will modify what she has already written. She likes for her emails to sound both friendly and eloquent. Finding the "right" words, according to her perfectionism, is different from accurately stating what she wants to say. Rather than focusing on the "right" words, she begins focusing on stating the point accurately and simply. She will also stop applying the same "right" and eloquent standard for writing to all emails and texts.

She will practice writing emails and text messages to friends and family without checking. She agrees that these emails and texts are low stakes, so if an error occurs, it will not affect someone's health.

Other ERP practices that she will implement include:

- Purposely writing a typo in a low-stakes email or text message

- Not proofreading low-stakes messages she writes

- Writing low-stakes messages quickly and without proofreading

- Purposely using incorrect words—such as four when she really means for, or their when it is correct to say there—on messages with low stakes

She agrees that although it will be difficult, she will not let anyone know she is purposely making errors, nor will she make a follow-up comment on her sent message to get reassurance that the recipient isn't judging her harshly. She knows that reassurance-seeking can be a way to feed obsessions and compulsions.

Gradually, Rebecca will work on time-limiting her work emails and proofing them just once. In addition, using her values as a guide, Rebecca decides to modify how much time she spends at work so she can spend quality time with her family too. She wants to start with taking a twenty-minute break to eat lunch at work, rather than working through lunchtime, and with leaving work by 6 p.m. every day.

Now it's your turn to use values as your guide and develop some ERP practices to modify your perfectionism. Think through some tasks, organize them into a menu, and begin your practice, using the guidelines in chapter 3.

Rather than fear driving your OCD, you may have sensory experiences associated with "not just right" experiences that drive your compulsions. Next, we will look at how you treat NJREs in OCD.

Treating NJREs in OCD

The focus of treating the NJREs in OCD is to do exposure that helps you practice tolerating the NJRE, and RP to gradually eliminate SOA and checking compulsions.

Let's look at Tim's experience:

I've got to have balance with everything. I quit wearing shoes with laces because I need to feel equal on each foot, and I got stuck trying to get them to look exactly the same. When I touch something with my right hand, I have to touch it with my left hand too, or I get an unequal feeling from the lack of balance and I don't feel right. I can't tolerate that NJRE in my body. I fear if I don't balance things out, I'll become dysfunctional from the NJRE. My stuff needs to look a certain way, and if things aren't even or symmetrical, I have to go rearrange it immediately to have it symmetrical, or I won't feel right. I'm afraid I could go crazy if I don't get relief from my NJREs.

Exposures that will help Tim include purposely provoking the NJR sensations by creating unequalness on one side of his body. Wearing shoes with laces that encourage him to confront the feelings that arise when they're not identical, and purposely touching something on one side and not the other, will help Tim practice having the NJR sensation and learning what happens if he stays with the feeling. Generally, he is triggered by asymmetry and unevenness in his environment, so he can make pictures on the wall uneven or arrange his books and belongings to appear asymmetrical. He might spend a set time looking at these visually triggering asymmetries and noticing his internal experience.

As with all ERP, Tim will practice a variety of exposure exercises with different triggers, and varying times to challenge the story his mind is telling him—that if he stays with the NJRE, he will go crazy. To target the NJR sensation, Tim can choose a time of day to wear two different types of shoes; put a weight in one pocket; part his hair differently so it feels "wrong"; wear two different types of socks; wear a single earring or a heavy watch or bracelet around one wrist; attach a hair clip on one side of his head; and touch something on one side and not the other. Whatever the exercise, Tim will approach it with curiosity and stay with the exposure for a predetermined time. It's recommended to stay with this kind of exposure for a minimum of one hour. Eventually, it will be helpful for him to make a regular practice of triggering the NJR sensation by wearing two different socks or a weight in his pocket that he leaves there all day while doing normal activities.

Finally, Tim might also practice exposures where he leaves something "wrong" in his surroundings that he will deal with not immediately, but whenever he happens to see it as he goes through his typical day. Once he practices this, he can also have someone surprise him by moving different objects that trigger the NJRE.

Over time, Tim will learn that he can tolerate the NJREs and won't go crazy or become dysfunctional. And to maintain his progress, he will continue to do daily ERP that targets his NJREs.

Points to Remember

Perfectionism can be a factor that maintains your OCD and can interfere with your progress, so it's important to look at how your perfectionism is functioning in your life. It's also entirely possible for you to transform unhelpful perfectionism to helpful perfectionism. Healthy perfectionism is meaningful and helps you live a fulfilling life; unhelpful perfectionism is driven by negativity and fear. Ask yourself if your perfectionism is moving you in the direction of living a fulfilling life. Ultimately, you'll use your values as a guide as you work toward prioritizing your efforts to achieve healthy perfectionism.

A subtype of OCD associated with perfectionism is focused on "not just right" experiences. If this type of OCD is a problem for you, exposure to NJREs will target the sensations you experience.

So far, you have learned a variety of skills to break the rules of OCD. More generalized ambient experiences, like shame and self-criticism, can contribute to your OCD maintenance cycle and the isolation that can be associated with it. The antidote to shame is self-compassion. In the next chapter, you will learn how self-compassion can help you in your recovery from OCD.

CHAPTER 10

Healing with Self-Compassion

In this chapter, we will address how to break the OCD rule *Keep your OCD hidden from others*. When you follow the rules of OCD, you most likely experience shame, guilt, and embarrassment that lead you to criticize yourself harshly and feel isolated from others. These can be barriers to successfully treating your OCD. You can learn to move from toxic shame and self-criticism to self-compassion. Self-compassion, both the concept and an active practice, can help you deactivate your anxiety when you are in a harmless situation and help you activate a feeling of security, trust, and calm (Gilbert and Tirch 2009).

What Drives the *Keep Your OCD Hidden from Others* Rule

Shame is a feeling based on an evaluation of yourself as being in some way broken, defective, or bad. Shame is a painful emotion that everyone experiences. It can be adaptive in some ways—that is, it can be a natural response when you've genuinely done something wrong and it leads you to correct your behavior so that it doesn't happen again. It can also become toxic. Experiencing shame is associated with anxiety and OCD

(Szentágotai-Tatar et al. 2020) and can lead to worsening of symptoms and the maintenance of your OCD cycle. It often leads to withdrawal from relationships and avoidance behaviors, and reinforces your obsessions and compulsions.

There is often particular stigma attached to disorders that affect your mental health, in both our surrounding or originating cultures and the wider societal contexts we find ourselves in. Shame about having a mental disorder—as well as some symptom-specific shame, like that which can be triggered by violent, sexual, or blasphemous obsessions—can lead you to secretiveness and isolation (Weingarden and Renshaw 2015). Shame can damage your relationships. Shame drives many to conceal their OCD symptoms from loved ones and treatment providers. Shame can also delay or prevent you from engaging in treatment for OCD.

Neuroscience research describes three emotional systems regulating human motivations that helped our ancestors survive: our threat system, which functions to help identify potential danger; our drive system, which motivates us to pursue goals; and our care system, which helps us feel content and calm (Gilbert 2009). In OCD, these systems are out of balance: the threat system is overactive and motivates compulsions to reduce fear as quickly as possible to feel safe. You may find yourself performing compulsions to neutralize shame. But as you know by now, compulsions can't bring you the feeling of safety you seek. What's more, when your threat system is overactive, it narrows your attention to dealing with threats and overrides other experiences and positive emotions. All the rules of OCD can directly or indirectly activate your brain's threat system, keeping it chronically overactive. And the harsh self-criticism that often accompanies shame and perfectionism can also keep your threat system overactive.

The media often portrays OCD in a way that minimizes the level of distress you feel. You may hear people around you say, "I'm a little bit OCD" and then proceed to tell you about how they have their closet color-coded or enjoy cleanliness. Have you ever walked into a store and seen a sweater emblazoned with something like "Obsessive Christmas

Disorder"? Popular culture's understanding of what having OCD is really like is woefully off-base. When you hear people make light of it, it can leave you feeling alone, broken, and misunderstood.

How This Rule Affects Your Life

Following the rule *Keep your OCD hidden from others* often leads to keeping secrets, isolating yourself, and feeling lonely. Let's look at some examples.

Eduardo says: "I was at a party with my family and noticed a man wearing a shirt that I really liked. Maybe this means I'm attracted to him. Maybe I'm gay or bisexual? I couldn't stand the feeling, so I went into the bathroom and stuck my finger up my asshole to see if I got sexually aroused. What kind of person does this? How shameful. I love my wife and children and we have a good relationship, but these experiences shake my confidence to shreds."

If Madison doesn't play a perfect basketball game, he fears he'll disappoint his team. *"Everyone might be really angry with me, I think, and I'll be asked to leave the team.* I get really anxious, and if I start worrying about whether I forgot to bring my lucky coin, I'm more likely to make a mistake. I'm so ashamed and angry with myself when I play poorly. I'm harder on myself than the coach is, and he's tough!"

JJ, parent of a toddler, finds she often has alarming thoughts about looking at her child's genitals in a sexual way. She finds herself mentally reviewing bath times, including how she felt and how her daughter responded to it, to figure out whether she's becoming a pedophile. She also feels intense shame and self-disgust at both her obsessions and her struggles with them. And the content she's struggling with feels so terrible that she worries she'll never be able to talk to anyone about it.

Yesterday, Tia was cutting vegetables and her daughter gave her a hug and asked for a carrot. She had an obsession that was accompanied with a strong impulse to stab her daughter. Now Tia thinks *Am I a monster?*

Joey says, "I'm not worthy of having the life I want, because OCD puts my loved ones through so much."

Darren feels ashamed when the police arrive to question him, in response to someone's call to report his behavior as suspicious. He had been carefully scrutinizing car tires in a parking lot in response to obsessions that maybe he'd accidentally punctured a tire; then he'd gone inside and blocked it out of his mind.

Zoe goes to confession for the fourth time that day, and the priest is upset by her repeatedly taking his time. Now she feels even more embarrassed, humiliated, and ashamed.

In all of these examples, people suffering from the OCD cycle are having thoughts and feelings that exacerbate their suffering, making it worse and sometimes harder to treat. Their OCD determines how they think others see them and how they feel about themselves.

Exercise: The *Keep Your OCD Hidden from Others* Rule

Reflect on how you follow this rule by identifying specific thoughts, compulsions, and avoidant behavior that you engage in. How does following this rule affect your quality of life and impact your ability to carry out the behaviors that really matter to you?

Now that you know the signs of following the rule *Keep your OCD hidden from others*, we'll address how to break it.

Breaking Free

Self-compassion practices are the antidote for shame and harsh self-criticism. Compassion is generally defined as a sensitivity to suffering in self and others, with a commitment to try to alleviate and prevent it (Gilbert 2022). The three components of self-compassion, in particular, are mindfulness, common humanity, and self-kindness (Neff 2011).

Mindfulness helps you observe your internal experiences and achieve present-moment awareness—awareness of your own suffering—without judgment. This can help you disentangle yourself from any harsh self-criticism that you experience, from the emotions that lead you to separate yourself and feel isolated in your struggle, and from the stories your OCD tells you, or the story you tell yourself about your OCD.

The story in your mind is likely that you are flawed and other people are better off than you are. It is important for you to understand that your experience of suffering is part of a larger human experience that we all share. OCD may look like an extreme form of suffering compared to what others' lives look like from the outside, but in reality, suffering is a continuum, and often people around you are experiencing more and tougher things than others can see from the outside.

It's not always easy to be this mindful, but once you have the capacity and an awareness of the universality of suffering and the humanity you share with other OCD sufferers and everyone else on earth, you can treat yourself and your OCD with care, kindness, and understanding rather than self-judgment.

Scientific studies on the effectiveness of practicing self-compassion are producing favorable findings related to health, well-being, and resilience (Neff et al. 2018). Practicing self-compassion is linked to improved mental health, with participants reporting less depression, anxiety, and stress (MacBeth and Gumley 2012). You are less likely to be gripped by anxiety when you train your mind in self-compassion. Compassionate mind practices can help you gain a healthier balance between your threat, drive, and care emotional regulation systems—the systems in your brain and body that help you respond to threats you might encounter (whether real or perceived), go after things you want, and care for yourself when you're suffering, respectively (Gilbert 2009). Thus developing a compassionate mind can help you move yourself more purposefully from your threat system to your care system where you can feel safe, encouraged, and content. Compassionate mind training also builds your capacity to engage in the suffering that can occur when you face your fears, and it helps you reduce excessive threat responding.

Ultimately, the energy of compassion can be nurturing or fierce. Your compassionate mind involves a tender side with comfort, soothing, and validating; it can also be fierce to protect, provide, and motivate. In the exercises that follow, we'll help you leverage both these sides of compassion as part of your effort to break the rules of OCD.

Tapping Into Your Compassionate Mind

There are many skills that can help you develop your compassionate mind. The following exercises will help you practice relating to yourself with compassion by cultivating and listening to your compassionate self—the part of you that is courageous, wise, encouraging, validating, patient, nonjudgmental, and kind.

As you practice self-compassion, you may find yourself feeling uncomfortable. When you learn to activate your care and soothing system, you may initially feel intense emotions that are unsettling to you. Sometimes self-compassion itself can feel like ERP.

It is important to support your body in a way that will help you move to your care system by noticing your posture. To experience your care system physiologically, in your body, you need to be in a posture where your spine is supported, shoulders are back, and chest is open. This is a posture that supports your breathing.

Soothing Touch

As humans, our earliest care involves physical touch by caregivers. One way of eliciting self-compassion is by experimenting with a physical touch you can provide to yourself that feels soothing. For some, a hand on their heart may feel soothing; for others, that may create anxiety. Placing your hands on your belly or stroking your arm or your face may be gestures that feel supportive.

Along with physical touch, humans communicate care through a soothing tone of voice. How does your tone of voice sound to you in your mind as you notice your thoughts? Begin adjusting your tone of voice to one that sounds soothing to you.

Exercise: Being Your Own Friend

Imagine a friend is suffering in some way and comes to you to share something challenging, a situation where your friend felt inadequate or like a failure. How do you respond to your friend? Notice the tone of your voice, words you would say, and nonverbal gestures you would use. Write this down.

Now think about a time when you experienced something challenging, when you felt inadequate or thought you failed. How did you respond to yourself in this situation? What did your mind say, and what tone of voice did your mind use? What was your posture, and what gestures did you use? Write this down.

How do you treat friends differently from yourself when it comes to dealing with life's challenges? Write this down.

Reflect on what you have learned in this exercise, based on "How Would I Treat a Friend?" (Germer and Neff 2019).

If you treat your friends with compassion and yourself with harsh self-criticism, you are not alone. As a person with OCD, you likely have higher levels of empathy and compassion for other people's suffering than for your own (Kämpf et al. 2022). Begin treating yourself as you would treat a friend, and notice what happens. This will take consistent practice and patience on your part, but if you can stick with it, you'll find it may be easier to deal with your OCD symptoms, practice effective ERP, be open about OCD and how it affects your life, and get the support you need, from others and from yourself.

Exercise: The Self-Compassion Break

The self-compassion break, developed by Germer and Neff (2019), is a practice you can use when you encounter moments of suffering. This practice includes the three aspects of compassion described by Neff (2011): mindfulness, common humanity, and self-kindness.

Your first step is to be present, noticing your suffering, and allowing it to be there without resisting it, rather than overidentifying with it.

When you notice your suffering, pause, and say to yourself *This is a moment of suffering.*

The second step is to remind yourself *I'm not alone; suffering is part of life.* This step will help you feel connected to common humanity rather than feeling isolated.

The last step is to practice self-kindness by giving yourself what you need at the time. Make a statement to yourself, such as *May I provide myself what I need.*

Alternative statements you may find helpful include:

- May I accept myself as I am.

- May I have strength.

- May I be patient.

- May I have courage.

- May I give myself compassion.

- May I learn from my experiences.

Practice the self-compassion break with words that most resonate with you. You can also experiment with using soothing touch while doing the self-compassion break.

At first, this practice may seem somewhat mechanical and contrived. Keep practicing. Also, experiment with using different words or different forms of soothing touch. And be aware of both your tone of voice in your mind and your posture. This exercise can easily be hijacked by your OCD and become a ritual. When you notice you're suffering and are tempted to use your self-kindness statement, pause for a moment. You can quickly assess whether you are using your statement to practice self-compassion or in a bid to avoid your discomfort.

From Self-Criticism to Self-Correction

Shaming self-criticism doesn't help you perform at your best, and it keeps your threat system overactive. That said, your inner self-critic does have a function that can serve you well when it is not driven by an overactive threat system. Ultimately, you can adjust the way your self-critic operates so you can make the most of your desire to do well (which we all have) without subjecting yourself to shaming self-criticism, which only makes life harder and more painful, rather than genuinely helping you improve.

Imagine that you are watching a special child in your life, Tara, play basketball in a championship tournament. She is passionate about the game and her basketball team. The score of the game is close, and Tara is not playing her best. You can see she is working hard and appears distressed. Her coach is yelling: "What's wrong with you, Tara? You missed another shot that a toddler could have made. You are a disgrace to your team and should be ashamed of yourself. You better not screw up again." Her team loses the game.

Do you notice any distressing internal experiences in response to what her coach said? Tara's threat system is overactivated, and she feels anxious about her next game. She has already developed a harsh self-critic that is as shaming as her coach.

Now consider another approach to coaching Tara when she isn't playing her best: "You've got this, you know what to do: Align your feet and watch your follow-through." After the tournament, too—not during the heat of play, when it might be stressful—Tara's coach could use compassionate correction to help her face her mistakes with self-kindness and encourage her to improve. The coach could validate her in her struggle, too, letting her know that "Even the best professional players make mistakes and lose games."

Shaming self-criticism, by contrast, is you focusing on attacking and punishing yourself. And when you are harsh with yourself, you attack your global sense of self. You may view your whole self as "broken" and feel discouraged. This leaves you afraid of failing again and half-convinced that you will, so you understandably respond with avoidance and withdrawal. Compassionate self-correction, on the other hand, focuses on helping yourself reflect compassionately on things that have happened and setting manageable goals going forward so you can genuinely improve. When you practice it, you feel encouraged and motivated to learn and grow. Learning and growing involve practicing new skills that may be challenging at first. To be motivated to practice challenging new skills, you need to feel secure, and compassion helps you give yourself that security; shame and self-criticism do not.

Exercise: Your Harsh Inner Critic

In your journal, write a description of a struggle in which your inner critic is harsh with you. It may be related to your OCD or not. Notice what your critic says and where you feel it in your body. What values are important to your inner critic?

Imagine what a compassionate coach would say to you in response to your struggle. In your journal, change your harsh self-criticism to compassionate correction. Notice any change in how you respond.

Compassionate Letter Writing

A wonderful way to cultivate your compassionate self is to write letters to yourself from a compassionate stance. As you are cultivating your compassionate self, it may be easiest to write your letter as though it's being sent to you from an imaginary compassionate being that is wise, courageous, encouraging, and kind. Eventually, as this begins to feel more natural, you can write your letters from the perspective of your compassionate self.

In your letter to yourself, write about a concern you have from the perspective of a nonjudgmental and loving friend who is validating and shares compassionate, wise thoughts. Make sure the tone expresses warmth, caring, and sensitivity to your feelings. Before beginning to write, pause, adjust your posture, slow down your breathing, and take some breaths for a couple of minutes. Consider structuring your letter in the following way:

1. Begin with a statement of concern that demonstrates sensitivity to your feelings.

2. Validate your feelings with openness.

3. Express that you are not alone.

4. Make a helpful statement that offers other perspectives on your concern.

5. Consider an action item that is a small step that moves you forward.

6. Add a compassionate phrase.

7. Close with a statement of appreciation or care.

In the previous section, you read about Tia and Eduardo's experience. Let's look at their self-compassion letters.

Dearest Tia,

I know you feel afraid that your intrusive thoughts, along with an urge to harm your daughter, make you a monster that may actually harm her. Your distress is understandable, because you are the most caring, gentle and loving mother that I know, and you want to protect your sweet daughter. You are not alone in having intrusive thoughts to harm your loved ones. Having disturbing thoughts is part of the human condition. You did a great job of embracing sweet Jenny and cutting her a carrot to eat. You demonstrated so much courage by practicing ERP. These triggers may come and go from time to time. Keep up the good work and know that I am with you always.

May you feel at peace.

In appreciation,

Your compassionate Tia

In the next example, see how you can use a self-compassion letter to learn from an experience that involves performing compulsions.

Dear Eduardo,

Dude, that was a rough night you had when you felt scared you might be gay. It's okay to feel afraid; everyone feels afraid sometimes. I know you are disappointed in yourself for giving in to your obsession by doing a checking compulsion in the bathroom at the dinner party. Nobody is perfect in their recovery from OCD, so be gentle with yourself right now. Bro, we don't get to choose our thoughts and sensations. Our brains are going to do what our brains do, and sometimes that creates suffering.

I want you to know I notice that sometimes you forget you are in charge. You'll experience OCD triggers, and that's not your fault. It's your responsibility to exercise your agency in how you respond to your distress. When you are triggered again, you could ask yourself *If I'm responding out of my best, most compassionate self that is following my values, what behaviors do I want to engage in?* OCD moments are likely to happen again, and you can use what you learned from that night to help you move forward. You are a caring, loving, and fun dude who enjoys family.

May you feel your strength, courage, and connection to others.

May you learn from your experiences.

Kind regards,

Your compassionate Eduardo

As you write self-compassion letters, address whatever it is you need right now. At times, your letter may simply show appreciation and care for you. At other times, your letter may encourage action that will move you toward something you are avoiding.

Compassionate Care for Your Body

As you ask yourself what you need each day, don't forget compassionate care for your body by getting restful sleep, exercise, and good nutrition. The basic things you do to take care of yourself and feel good are also expressions of self-compassion.

Take a moment to assess, in your journal, how you're doing with self-care in each of the following domains. Are there any new behaviors or practices you could try?

- Exercise: Are you exercising regularly? Even a moderate amount of regular exercise counts. It doesn't need to be intense; something as simple as a long walk or the occasional stretching session could be useful.

- Sleep: Are you getting adequate sleep each night?

- Relaxation: Do you regularly practice activities that calm and soothe you? Exercise might be one, or you might try a regular practice of time in nature, time spent with family or friends, or restorative activities like art, reading a good book, listening to calming music, and more.

- Nutrition: Are you eating regularly, and in ways that help you feel nourished?

Self-Compassion and ERP

As you go through your daily life, when you feel anxious, frustrated, or uncomfortable, practice self-compassion. Begin with *What do I need right now?* Your compassionate self may give you courage that helps you with your ERP. Before doing your ERP, do some self-compassion practices to tap into your compassionate self; this can help you feel more secure as you face your fears during exposure. During exposure, allow your compassionate self to provide wise coaching if you need it; once you have completed your exposure task, it can validate your experience. Give yourself whatever you need at the time from your compassionate self. There are many skills that can help you develop your compassionate self.

The key is to remember that the practice of compassion is about strength and courage, because it represents our ability to turn to face our suffering. And remember, your sense of self-compassion is like a muscle; the more you use it, the stronger and better developed it becomes.

Points to Remember

Self-compassion can help you achieve balance in your three emotional regulation systems. As you struggle with your OCD, your threat system is overactivated in contexts where there aren't current threats. Shame and harsh self-criticism engage your threat system unnecessarily. You can dial back your self-critic and provide yourself with compassionate self-correction. Self-compassion practices are always available to you and can help you achieve better well-being. It may take time for you to feel the positive effects of self-compassion practices.

Moving forward, it is important for you to establish daily compassion practices. When you engage in compassion, you are moving from your overactive threat system to your soothing system where you feel safe. Your compassionate self can help you move through your OCD triggers and do ERP consistently.

We have barely scratched the surface of the multiple paths you can take to practice self-compassion in your daily life. For a thorough review—whether your initial practices with self-compassion seem helpful or you find you're struggling with it—see *The Self-Compassion Workbook for OCD* by Kimberley Quinlan.

CHAPTER 11

Optimizing and Maintaining Your Progress

In this chapter, we will address how you can maximize the effectiveness of your ERP practices. We'll also address common challenges you may encounter and review guidelines for successful ERP.

You have learned a variety of practices to help you break the rules and move beyond your OCD. You have learned mindfulness, curiosity, willingness, and self-compassion practices that not only assist you during ERP but also help enrich your life. These practices also help you end the fight with your symptoms by allowing discomfort. It is when you fight with unwanted thoughts, feelings, and sensations that these uncomfortable experiences take control of you.

Chances are, some of the practices you have learned in this book have worked better than others at helping you break free from the grip of OCD. OCD manifests in many different ways, and there are many ways to approach ERP practices to help optimize its potential. To maintain your progress, it's helpful to experience and practice a large repertoire of skills; this will increase your capacity to let anxiety be present while you freely engage in your life as you wish.

In this next section, we will take a deeper dive into adding more variety to your ERP to optimize what you learn from it.

Boost Your ERP

Recent research in fear learning has provided new insights into how we can maximize effectiveness with ERP. In this section, we will let Doug's experience with OCD illustrate using these principles.

Doug's Story

Doug's sister, Helen, sustained injuries in an accident and will spend the rest of her life using a wheelchair. While training for a bicycle race on February 21st, she was hit by a drunk driver. Doug became fearful that something life threatening would happen to his loved ones. Doug started checking in with his wife throughout the day to see if she was okay, and when he didn't get an immediate response, he would hyperventilate as he thought of terrible things that could happen to her.

Doug's motto became "better safe than sorry," so to prevent harm, he started avoiding triggers that reminded him of the accident. He avoided the intersection where the accident occurred and eventually couldn't drive anywhere near the bike path she'd been on. The drunk driver was from Oklahoma, so when Doug saw an Oklahoma license plate he would sweat, feel queasy, and begin hyperventilating. As time passed, the 21st of each month was associated with danger; he'd think, Someone might die. Eventually he was fearful of any appearance of a 21, or a 12, or a 221. He thought it was dangerous to do anything important on the 12th, 21st, and at the time 2:21. He associated his intrusive images of Helen's wounds with the color red. He threw away his and his wife's red clothing. He feared that if he was around these triggers, he would "catch" bad luck and something terrible would happen. Doug began carrying a traveler's prayer coin in his pocket and gave each family member one for good luck.

Notice how Doug's danger associations with the accident expanded from the specific intersection where the accident happened to the drunk driver's home state, from the date it happened to varied appearances of the numbers 2 and 1, and from his sister's wounds to the color red in general. As mentioned in chapter 3, your brain learns to develop fear associations, and even when your brain learns through ERP, your fear associations are not erased. By using ERP, though, Doug can create new learning about these triggers that will help inhibit the fear learning. With time and practice, fear learning weakens and is replaced with new, non-threatening associations. Doug will eventually learn that the intersection, Oklahoma, the numbers 2 and 1, and the color red aren't dangerous. He does so by structuring his ERP according to certain principles that enhance inhibitory learning.

These principles for enhancing inhibitory learning, proposed by Craske et al. (2014), include catch phrases that are easy to remember: test it out, vary it up, combine it, talk it out, stay with it, throw it out, and bring it back. Let's apply each of these principles to Doug's ERP; then you can use them to develop additional ERP practices for yourself.

Test It Out

The goal in designing exposures that will *test it out* is to optimize the discrepancy between what you expect or fear will happen, and what actually happens. Neuroscience research suggests that your learning is maximized when your experience doesn't match what you predict will happen. Doug fears he'll catch bad luck when encountering triggers. For example, Doug predicts that:

- *If I see or hear anything that has to do with Oklahoma, something bad will happen to a loved one.*

- *If I do an important task at 2:21, something terrible will happen to a loved one.*

- *If I encounter the color red, someone I know will die.*

- *If I do any of these exposures, my anxiety will be so intolerable, I will be inconsolable and have to be hospitalized.*

Doug develops the following exposures:

- Listen to music from the musical *Oklahoma!* for thirty minutes each day.

- Place an online order at precisely 2:21 each day.

- Use a red marker to write a note to someone each day for a week.

Prior to exposure, Doug estimated the likelihood of something bad happening to a loved one, if he saw or heard anything to do with Oklahoma or did an important task at 2:21 p.m., to be 75 percent. The first exposure he is willing to do is to order something online at 2:21 each day. As you implement ERP, it is a prerequisite that you agree to completing the exposure without performing any compulsions, and that's what Doug will do.

Each day, once he completes the exposure, he summarizes his experience. He feels anxious and has queasy sensations in his stomach when he inputs information to complete his online order at 2:21. After that, he writes about his experience: his obsession didn't come true, and his anxiety did subside after an hour. It was also much easier to tolerate than he expected. He did experience what-if thoughts that came and went throughout the afternoon and at bedtime.

Can you identify exposures that you have done or that you can do to *test it out* and see what happens? Note: It's crucial to reflect on what you learned from each ERP session and write it down.

Also, be aware of any attempts your mind makes to convince you that your fear is unlikely to occur as a way of convincing yourself that it is worth it to do ERP. That's not the kind of persuasion you want to use. Any cognitive tool that you use can weaken the effect of your learning.

Vary It Up

Safety learning can't be generalized to all situations, so it is important for you to conduct your exposures in a variety of ways. Do ERP in different locations, at different times of day, and with varied stimuli, interpersonal contexts, and emotional states. You need to be able to respond flexibly to your obsessions when you are tired, stressed, anxious, sad, happy; when you're alone as well as when others are around. So you need to practice ERP when you have different emotional and energy states, as well as alone and with others nearby.

You can also vary the exposure intensity and choose an exposure that is more challenging rather than moving gradually.

Once you have practiced one exposure successfully and consistently over time, you can vary your practice interval by spacing out when you do your ERP. For example, Doug could place different online orders at 2:21 several days apart and see what happens.

Can you think of a variety of ways that Doug could do ERP with the color red? He can purchase a red rose for his wife, hold it in his hand for a while, and give it to her. He could put a red scarf around his neck or wear red socks. He could even take his family to dinner at the Red Lobster restaurant. Working with the color red when he has an important business meeting or when relaxing alone would offer some added variety. He could also make a list of exposures that vary in intensity and choose one randomly to introduce variation that way. This could be done by numbering them and rolling some dice to choose the exposure.

Now it's your turn. Write down some ideas for how you can implement adding variety to your ERP. How can you *vary it up?*

Combine It

Once you have completed exposure tasks successfully, you can combine two tasks to deepen your learning. Consider triggers in your external environment, such as people, objects, contaminants, and locations, and your internal environment, such as your thoughts, feelings, memories, or sensations. Now design exposures that either combine one or more triggers that you have already worked on individually or add a new exposure to one you have already worked on. You can combine exposure to your external environment with imaginal and/or interoceptive exposure.

Doug could combine listening to a music playlist from the musical *Oklahoma!* or music from artists who are from Oklahoma while doing interoceptive exposure to experience hyperventilation, sweating, and queasiness in his stomach. He could listen to music from *Oklahoma!* while doing something important at 2:21. He could order red clothing or objects at 2:21 online.

Now it's your turn to write some ideas of how you can *combine it* in your own exposure.

Talk It Out

Verbally expressing your emotions helps you develop new associations. And when you verbalize an emotion, you are activating a part of the brain associated with inhibitory learning. In other words, labeling the emotions you experience during an exposure can facilitate its effects. During your exposure, use a feeling word that best describes your emotional experience as well as a descriptive word for what you are afraid of.

When Doug wears a pair of red socks, he might verbalize his emotions during exposure by saying something like, "I feel afraid. I feel that the red socks that remind me of blood will bring bad luck to my loved ones."

Now it's your turn. How can you add descriptions of your emotions to *talk it out* during your exposure?

Stay with It

To boost the effectiveness of ERP, focus on the most disturbing part of the exposure. This will enhance learning by maximizing the difference between what you expect to happen and what actually happens. During exposure, pay deliberate attention to your experience with what you are targeting along with your thoughts, feelings, and sensations. It is only natural that your mind will divert attention away from your exposure target. When you notice you are distracted, simply notice that and keep your awareness on the most disturbing part of the exposure. Staying with it is hard and takes a lot of practice—one good reason to regularly and consistently practice your mindfulness skills.

When Doug engages in exposure, he focuses on bad luck that can occur to his family and *stays with it*.

Now it's your turn. How can you *stay with it* during ERP?

Throw It Out

Safety signals and behaviors can weaken your ERP and interfere with learning. You can boost your ERP by removing safety behaviors. These can be people, objects, places, and superstitions that signal safety. Objects frequently used as safety behaviors include hand sanitizer, wipes, cell phones, water, and certain clothing. Keeping the air conditioning on or having a fan nearby can also be a safety behavior.

When it comes to practicing this principle, Doug could remove the traveler's prayer coin he carries in his pocket for good luck and leave it at home when he goes out.

Now it's your turn. What safety signals and behaviors can you eliminate for ERP? Begin by asking yourself what you avoid, or what you do that makes you think your feared outcome is less likely to occur. Are there any objects that make you think your feared outcome is less likely?

Toward the end of your therapy, you can use the following strategy to *bring it back*.

Bring It Back

This strategy is one to use only after you have experienced a lot of successful ERP practices. To bring back the experience, you can think of memories of successful exposures or use a cue that symbolizes prior success with your exposure to help prevent relapse. Your new learning during ERP may weaken over time, and your fear associations may return. You can help your brain remember your new learning by recalling an exposure practice that went well, then practice bringing the memory back as vividly as you can. Verbalize what you learned from your exposure as part of this practice. When you encounter a new situation that triggers you, bring into your mind a vivid memory of the success you had with a previous exposure prior to doing exposure in a new situation. You could put a picture that represents a memory of successful exposure on your refrigerator or have an object that symbolizes successful exposures. Or you could post a reminder with a memory of your success with exposure in your cell phone.

In Doug's case, before doing exposure to a new experience, he could remember his experience of purposely placing an online order at 2:21.

A word of caution: *bring it back* can easily backfire and become a safety signal rather than the intended reinstatement of learning that your fear associations are safe. Be aware that you could use it inappropriately, as a reassurance ritual. So keep in mind exactly why you're using any intervention that you use. If you notice that you begin using it as a safety behavior, stop using that strategy.

Now it's your turn. What can you do to *bring it back*? Do you have an idea of what you might notice if you were using this as a safety signal instead of as a way to *bring it back*?

If you find challenges in working with any of the practices in this book, know that you are not alone. Be patient with yourself. OCD is tricky, so ERP may require experimenting with different approaches. And the practice is always evolving; there are some principles that can augment ERP for anxiety disorders and enhance outcomes. Several research studies are under way as of this writing to determine still better ways to apply these principles to OCD, so you can expect that over the next few years, we'll have even more ways to increase your chances of maximizing inhibitory learning with your ERP. Even now, as you proceed with ERP, you have a variety of ways to plan your exposures to maximize learning.

Next, we will look at some common challenges you may encounter when practicing ERP.

Common Challenges

In this section, we'll cover a few of the common challenges you might face as you continue on your journey with ERP:

- Co-occurring psychiatric illnesses

- Unrealistic expectations about the progress you might make and how quick it will be

- Lack of awareness of subtle rituals that can interfere with inhibitory learning

- Inconsistent practice of ERP

- Reassurance you might seek or get from people around you

- Use of ERP itself as a compulsion

Co-occurring Psychiatric Illnesses

This is an extremely common issue that can often interfere with a person's progress doing ERP for OCD. Two-thirds of people who have OCD also have a co-occurring disorder (Sharma et al. 2021). The most prominent co-occurring problems are mood disorders, anxiety disorders, personality disorders, and substance use disorders. Eating disorders, PTSD, ADHD, and tic disorders as well as other disorders in the obsessive-compulsive spectrum family, such as body dysmorphic disorder and trichotillomania, can commonly co-occur.

If you have not been screened for other conditions that may impact your functioning, consult with a doctor. Psychiatrists, in particular, specialize in treating psychiatric conditions and can help screen for other conditions you may have. A psychiatrist can also offer you medical options for your OCD and other co-occurring conditions. Ultimately, the scope of this book is to provide you with CBT skills, the first-line treatment for OCD—but medication, along with CBT, can also be very effective. If you are not on medication for your OCD and find yourself struggling with the practices in this book, schedule a consultation with a psychiatrist.

If you are having difficulty implementing the practices in this book, consult a therapist who specializes in treating OCD with CBT. It is crucial that you find a therapist who has training in providing specialized care and understands ERP. The International OCD Foundation (IOCDF) is the best resource to point you in the right direction. The IOCDF offers a lot of programs as well as a warm, caring community.

If you have found a particular OCD rule challenging to break, you may need the help of additional interventions. For example, if you struggle with perfectionism, you may benefit from adding CBT interventions specifically designed for perfectionism. If you find yourself fighting with your symptoms, adding more ACT or mindfulness practices may help. Another therapy to consider from the CBT family is inference-based CBT for OCD, which addresses your reasoning process.

Sometimes inadequate therapy impacts how much progress you can make. Some people may need intensive therapy, ranging from several times a week to participation in a specialized residential program.

Unrealistic Expectations

It's common for people to think that ERP doesn't work that well because of unrealistic expectations for how fast they can make progress and what their progress will look like. Many factors can affect how quickly you make progress. Severity, co-occurring mental health challenges, how long you have suffered from OCD, life circumstances, support from others, and how you are practicing ERP all can make a difference in how fast you improve. Some clients make some improvement within three months, and some take several years of consistent work. Ultimately, what helps here is patience, persistence, and a dedication to doing the things you care about, to buoy you when exposure gets difficult.

Values also matter when it comes to the belief that anxiety is dreadful and dangerous, which often manifests with OCD. Adhering to this belief will keep your focus on anxiety reduction rather than getting better at having anxiety and doing what you care about even though you're uncomfortable. Focusing on signs that you've reduced your anxiety paradoxically keeps you anxious. When you use values as your guide, your relationship with your discomfort changes.

Not Recognizing Subtle Rituals

This lack of awareness can also impede your progress. Sometimes you may find yourself in autopilot when responding to an obsession, or you may have subtle rituals that you don't realize are compulsions. You may also have symptoms that you purposely conceal because you feel ashamed, guilty, or embarrassed. You may have safety behaviors that seem reasonable and don't take extra time. For example, Timothy justifies walking with his hands in his pockets because he can move through his day without being tormented with thoughts like *Did I accidentally touch someone inappropriately while walking to my office?* Karen carries wipes and a bottle of water in her handbag just in case she touches something gross. The problem with safety behaviors is that your mind is continuing to think something that isn't dangerous is, and this keeps your behavior inflexible. Other subtle rituals are mental: For example, you may use searches for additional information as a reassurance ritual so you can move on with your day.

Inconsistent Practice

How you approach your ERP can limit your progress in several ways. Inconsistent practice of ERP is quite common. When you initially begin ERP, it is important to be intentional and consistent in your practice. There are times that you may do the exposure part of the ERP but not the response prevention part. Exposure without response prevention won't gain you the progress you seek.

You may sometimes find yourself experiencing extremely high anxiety during exposure, and feeling overwhelmed. If this happens, do your best to follow through with your RP plan and not do a compulsion. Remember, your anxiety isn't dangerous, and even though you feel overwhelmed, you are strong enough to allow the anxiety to be there while you engage in important activities. It's an opportunity to teach your mind that feeling overwhelmed is uncomfortable but not dangerous. You can observe your anxiety and ask yourself *Who is the person I want to be in this moment?* Act based on that, rather than on the easiest way to reduce your anxiety.

Sometimes you may discover that you have done ERP without its targeting your particular obsession. Go back to chapter 2, on identifying the function of your behavior with your OCD maintenance cycle. What is your trigger, how did you respond, and what was the result? If you are doing exposure to things that are germy and not washing your hands afterward, if germs aren't what you fear, then you may not benefit from the exposure. If you wash your hands because you feel disgust with bodily fluids, unless you fear that the germy surface has bodily fluids on it, it's unlikely to help.

Seeking and Getting Reassurance That Maintains Your OCD Cycle

You may also need to examine the function of what you are doing in the area of reassurance. You may easily think that you are simply educating yourself about a concern but find yourself spending hours with online searches that are really reassurance compulsions.

Relationships with others can affect your progress in many ways. If your family has learned to function better by anticipating your triggers and eliminating them for you, or by participating in your rituals so you can move through normal activities, this can delay your making the progress that you want. You may engage in seeking reassurance from your relationships so you can move on.

Others can inadvertently help you stay symptomatic. Loved ones can engage in behavior to try and help you or to avoid conflicts. If loved ones' behavior makes it easier for you to engage in rituals, it will be more difficult for you to practice new behaviors. Consider the following questions:

- Do you repeatedly ask for reassurance from others?

- Do you insist that loved ones participate in rituals?

- Do you encourage loved ones to avoid things that you are afraid of?

- Do your loved ones change their plans or behaviors to avoid upsetting you?

- Do your loved ones take on extra duties so that you aren't stressed?

- Do loved ones do anything that makes it easier for you to ritualize (purchasing supplies, doing your laundry, and so on)?

Placing an emphasis on your obsessions can get you hooked into the content of your thoughts. When this happens, your mind will attempt to use logic, and you'll argue with yourself.

ERP Itself Becoming a Compulsion

Your exposures can become compulsions in many ways. (Nothing is simple, is it?) If you have a sense of urgency to do ERP so that you can feel better, you may be making the decision so you can make OCD "go away." This is a tricky way that your mind can resist your discomfort and treat it like a problem to be solved. On the surface, it appears that you are doing something positive for yourself. To address this, you can shift to simply observing your internal experiences coming and going. Remember that the goal in ERP is to make contact with your anxiety, not expressly to reduce it. Return to carrying out your ERP practices when you don't have the sense of urgency to use it for anxiety reduction.

Not being fully present during ERP interferes with learning. Sometimes zoning out, thinking of other things, or engaging in subtle rituals can be ways of resisting being all-in with the ERP. You may notice some signs of resistance in your body sensations. Are you clenching your jaw, closing your eyes, holding your breath, or clenching your knuckles? Once you recognize that you are not present, tell yourself *Excellent noticing* and gently return to being present during your ERP practice.

Guidelines for Successful ERP

Now let's look at some general guidelines for successful ERP practice. Many of my clients have found it helpful to display these on their refrigerator, mirror, or bulletin board. A printable version can be found at http://www.newharbinger.com/51024.

Plan your ERP. Plan daily practices that work with your lifestyle. Set reminders for yourself to do your ERP. You may want to set alerts on your phone, use a prop or sticky notes, or have small stickers placed in strategic places where you want to remember to do ERP. Once you have consistently worked on a particular target and been successful, vary the time interval and time of day of your ERP practice.

Take a "bring it on" attitude. Embrace the opportunity to face your fears. You are stronger than you think, and more capable than you realize. Dealing with OCD is hard, and you are the one in charge. Find opportunities to implement ERP. The more you do, the more flexible and confident you will become to own your life and do what is important to you.

Identify your values. OCD has narrowed your thoughts and behaviors. This has prevented you from doing what matters most. Use your values as a compass to move toward a more meaningful life. Holding your values in mind can give you strength and motivation to do your ERP.

Have willingness to fully experience your fears and discomfort. Your compulsions and avoidance of anxiety have not allowed you to learn that you can cope with your discomfort. Be curious about what you experience while not engaging in rituals or avoidant behavior. Be all-in with your ERP.

Stay in contact with the present moment. Mental time travel to the past and future could scare you out of doing exposures. If you notice yourself mentally time traveling, gently bring yourself back to the present moment and welcome what feelings show up.

Expect to feel anxious and uncomfortable. The more you practice, the stronger you'll get. The stronger you get, the more flexible you become. The more flexible you become, the more freely you can move through each day.

Observe your thoughts, feelings, and sensations without interpretation. Get curious about what you are experiencing internally while noticing the feelings, thoughts, and sensations. Don't try to figure it out or explain what's going on; just observe and take it in as you feel it.

Allow fear to be present without fighting it. You can surf the ups and downs of the waves of your anxiety. Don't push your emotions away. Doing that just makes OCD thoughts rebound more strongly in your mind. Discomfort is dynamic and changes from moment to moment. You can fully accept whatever discomfort shows up.

Seek out uncertainty. Practice your "don't know" mind by allowing questions to remain unanswered. Notice with curiosity what it's like to leave questions unanswered.

Treat the content of your OCD thoughts as irrelevant. The OCD storyteller in your mind is creative and sneaky. Don't reply to the content of your obsessions. Replying returns you to your OCD cycle, which leads to avoidance and compulsions. You may find yourself experiencing analysis paralysis.

Keep in mind your metric for measuring success. The metric of success isn't anxiety reduction, but tolerating your anxiety. Pursue meaningful activities even while you're anxious, and welcome the discomfort that shows up.

Hold your shame, guilt, and self-criticism in a compassionate way. You can be the brave and kind friend that your anxious self needs.

Points to Remember

ERP is a powerful intervention. And, just as OCD can be tricky, so can ERP. You'll likely find some ERP exercises more effective for you than others, so it is important to practice a variety of ERP exercises; that way, you can discover the ones that work best for you. Also, although it is natural to use anxiety reduction as a metric for success, a much better metric for success with ERP is moving more flexibly in your life toward what matters to you, whatever you happen to be feeling. Ultimately, anxiety, thoughts, emotions, and sensations are not within your control. All thoughts, emotions, and sensations are part of normal brain functioning. And each person's journey of recovery will look different and happen at a different pace.

In the next chapter, we will address how to live beyond your OCD by adopting a CBT lifestyle.

CHAPTER 12

Living Beyond Your OCD

In this chapter, we will address how to live free from your OCD, over your lifetime, by adopting a CBT lifestyle—one in which you regularly use the principles of CBT to live in ways that challenge the rules OCD will try to hold you to. Continuing to practice breaking the rules of OCD with the skills you are learning from this book will require regular practice of ERP. As your relationship with your OCD changes over time, you may find yourself feeling anxious about what to do with your time, and you may experience grief over losses you experience because of your OCD. Dealing with the messiness of the human condition can be challenging and triggering to your OCD. But rest assured that you can live your life with passion while anxiety comes along for the ride.

What changes have you noticed in yourself since you started breaking the rules of OCD? Let's look at some signs of progress that you may notice:

- Sensing an improved quality of life

- Functioning with more effectiveness and satisfaction in important life areas, such as relationships, career or school, leisure, health, and spirituality

- Flexibly responding to your discomfort, rather than rigidly adhering to the rules of OCD

- Engaging in activities that are important to you

- Tolerating anxiety and uncertainty more readily

- Having more present-moment awareness rather than living on autopilot

- Noticing a different, easier relationship with your thoughts

- Enjoying better relationships with others

- Feeling more resilient

- Engaging in fewer avoidance behaviors, compulsions, or safety behaviors

Notice there's nothing among these signs of progress about eliminating anxiety and uncertainty. Your brain's job is to keep you alive, and to do that, you'll feel a full range of emotions, thoughts, and sensations—some of which are unpleasant. Fear is important for your survival, and you can continue learning to recognize when the threat system in your mind is overworking. Remember, a better metric for success than "not feeling anxiety" is making choices to do what matters to you *with* anxiety by your side. As you continue with values-based moves, your life will feel more meaningful.

And adopting a CBT lifestyle will help you continue to live life more flexibly.

Living a CBT Lifestyle

A CBT lifestyle involves making ERP part of your life as you move toward, rather than away from, situations that trigger your obsessions (Abramowitz 2018). If you are experiencing triggers of your OCD, it's important to practice ERP regularly. When you no longer experience anxiety during your ERP and are responding to your obsessions flexibly, following your RP plan, you can gradually reduce the frequency of your ERP. But when you follow the rules of OCD, over time you get conditioned to a way of responding to your discomfort with avoidance and compulsions that can range from being obvious to you and others around you to being subtle, sneaky, and difficult to identify.

Invite opportunities to get out of your comfort zone in areas of your life that are not affected by your OCD. This can be done when you learn something new, make new friends, eat at a new restaurant, or take a new route to run errands. Whether these examples seem like a welcome adventure or risky because the outcome is unknown, strive to practice being out of your comfort zone consistently with curiosity. These experiences will help you learn that you are stronger than you think, and that you can trust yourself.

Exercise: Progress Reflection

Reflect on the progress you have made so far in breaking the rules of OCD. What OCD behaviors have you eliminated? What skills have helped the most so far? What ERP do you need to continue? Where else can you go out of your comfort zone?

In addition to regularly practicing ERP, important elements of living a CBT lifestyle include living mindfully, acceptance, self-compassion, staying unhooked by your OCD stories, living according to your values, and staying connected to others. These elements help you respond flexibly to your internal and external environment.

Living mindfully is living in the present moment. As you've no doubt experienced over the course of your ERP, there is a space between when your obsessions arise and how you choose to respond. Without awareness of your obsession in the moment it occurs, you may be on autopilot and perform the compulsion that is conditioned behavior. You need present-moment awareness to exercise your agency and choose behaviors that will help you thrive.

Living mindfully will also enrich your experiences. When you find yourself encountering a trigger, rather than going on autopilot and doing what you have always done, you'll pause to notice what you are experiencing, so you can pivot in a direction that matters to you—and to observe all that is present in your environment, not just what OCD directs your attention to. Practice your informal mindfulness skills daily, experiment with a variety of formal meditation practices, and see what helps. Mindful attention is often difficult for people with OCD, so start slowly, with short practices. Consider setting up a regular chime on your phone as a reminder to take time to pause for a mindful moment.

The next part of a CBT lifestyle is acceptance: allowing or staying open to internal experiences even when you are uncomfortable. Your OCD gets stronger when you resist discomfort, and it loses its strength when you accept your uncomfortable internal experiences. As you practice the principles of aikido, you leave your OCD nothing to resist against. You may find your anxiety increasing temporarily, but you will feel more freedom to direct your energy to endeavors that are fulfilling to you. Keep in mind that everyone lives with discomfort, a full range of emotions, and uncertainty.

To summarize what we have discussed throughout this book, living a CBT lifestyle involves accepting the following:

- Suffering is part of life for everyone.

- You, like everyone, will have unpleasant internal experiences.

- Everyone lives with uncertainty.

- Like everyone, you will have unpleasant thoughts.

- Life is messy for everyone.

- You have OCD.

- Setbacks are a natural part of living with OCD.

- Recovery is possible.

- Practice and hard work are important.

- Life isn't fair.

- You, like everyone, will make mistakes.

- If you continue repeating the same behaviors, you'll continue experiencing the same outcomes.

- Just like anything worthwhile in life, recovery involves hard work, patience, persistence, and regular practice.

- If you can manage these things, you'll succeed in living your values and improving your quality of life.

Another important ingredient in all this is self-compassion. Having OCD is hard and you may feel alone and broken. It isn't easy to be patient with yourself and stay persistent when recovery isn't going your way. But remember: Behavior change is hard for everyone. Practicing self-compassion will help you bounce back more easily; cultivating a compassionate mind also takes time and practice. It is worthwhile for you to make compassion for yourself and others daily a part of living a CBT lifestyle; you'll also need to work at it a bit, especially when your OCD stories rear their heads to hook you again.

You are conditioned to naturally avoid your triggers and respond to them with compulsions. Do you find yourself easily triggered to perform compulsions because you deem that the stakes for the obsessional content are too high? It is common for anyone with OCD to find it challenging to choose ERP over giving in to the obsession. Again, you can do it! And the more you do, the stronger you will feel.

Your thoughts can become OCD storylines and develop into full-blown elaborate and frightening stories. Your relationship with the OCD storyteller in your mind can make a difference for you in your recovery. If you get caught up in trying to eliminate your OCD thoughts, you'll find yourself fighting them, which only gives them strength. Your OCD knows your vulnerabilities and gives you thoughts that are seductive. But part of living a CBT lifestyle is knowing that you are in charge of your response to your mind. Use your mindfulness here; practice noticing thoughts and observing them so you are not entangled by them. When you try to respond to your thoughts and resolve them, that can lead you to perform compulsions. Nevertheless, even when thoughts are alarming and sound important, you can practice observing them without being hooked by the disturbing content. You can coexist with your OCD and tolerate your obsessions as part of recovery.

Finally, as you make behavioral choices, use your values as your guide. What choices move you toward the life that is important to you? You may feel a strong pull to move away from your unwanted internal experiences. Rather than move away from discomfort, move *toward* what is important to you, and carry your discomfort with you.

One last note (it bears repeating): As you put these principles into action every day, and build yourself a CBT lifestyle, it'll be important to take good care of yourself by getting the physical exercise, nutrition, and sleep that you need. This is foundational for good health.

Exercise: Creating a Personal Pledge

In your notebook, or using the downloadable form from http://www.newhar-binger.com/51024, create a personal pledge to yourself outlining what you'll strive to do each day to live a CBT lifestyle. A pledge to yourself is an intention you state that orients you to what matters in a supportive way. To keep your pledge meaningful to you, include the following:

- Living mindfully

- Facing your fears

- Acceptance

- Self-compassion

- Your relationship with your thoughts

- Taking actions according to your values

For example:

I want to live my life free from OCD.

Today, I pledge that I will live mindfully by setting a timer to do a three-minute meditation, and when I notice that I feel anxious, I will pause before responding.

Today, I pledge to face my fears by doing ERP.

Today, I pledge to accept my uncomfortable thoughts, feelings, and sensations.

Today, I pledge to practice cultivating my compassionate mind by doing the self-compassion break.

Today, I pledge to observe my thoughts as they come and go.

Today, I pledge to take action in the service of my values by taking my children to the park to play.

Today, I pledge to embrace my mistakes as a chance to learn.

Revisit your pledge as often as you need to, to help keep yourself on track with your ERP and your behavior-change efforts.

Handling Setbacks

A setback is an increase of symptoms associated with your OCD. Setbacks in progress are a natural part of the recovery process; everyone will experience them from time to time. You can learn a lot from your setbacks; treating each as a learning opportunity will help you get through it more easily. It's a common reaction to feel disappointed and demoralized and blame yourself, and to think I'm back to square one; now I have to start over or I might as well give up; recovery is too much work if it isn't going to stick.

Keep in mind that recovery from OCD isn't a slope where the trend involves a gradual disappearance of symptoms. A slope of recovery looks different for everyone. At times it has the characteristic of a sawtooth; sometimes it's more like a flat line, or a line that moves up and down gradually. Many variables may go into experiencing setbacks in progress, for example:

- Difficulty being consistent with living a CBT lifestyle

- Psychiatric or physical illness

- Accidents

- Environmental disasters

- World challenges, such as pandemics, economic adversity, and social injustice

- Life changes

Regardless of whether a life change is a positive, welcome event, such as getting married, having a baby, buying a home, or getting a job promotion, or unwelcome changes, like death of a loved one, illness, divorce, or job loss, change is stressful, and you'll be dealing with uncertainty and unknowns. Change is always happening, and some of it may trigger your symptoms.

When you encounter a setback, practice self-compassion. Revisit the chapters on the OCD maintenance cycle to see how OCD is affecting you now, and return to practicing ERP. Your mind may develop a negative narrative about your setback that will add to feelings of discouragement, demoralization, or shame. Remember that how you respond to your mind can make a huge difference. Practice observing your thoughts and not getting entangled by the content. Make decisions from your wise, compassionate mind. Once you are back on track, you'll be in a better state of mind to learn from your experience. This may involve compassionate correction of behaviors that may have contributed to the setback, or learning more about yourself that may help you with altering your lifestyle if necessary.

Since we are all imperfect and everyone's life is messy, it is useful for you to identify potential vulnerabilities that can contribute to setbacks so you can stay observant and make decisions that help keep you on track.

Exercise: My Red Flags

In your journal, write down your answers to the following prompts:

1. Make a list of red flags—warning signs that include high-risk situations, environments, thoughts, feelings, and sensations that can trigger your OCD. Examples: certain numbers, colors, contaminants, public places, weapons.

2. Make a list of thoughts you have about yourself that make you feel vulnerable to getting entangled with your OCD. Examples: "I'm not good enough, I'm disgusting, I'm immoral, I might be a pedophile, I might kill a loved one, I might be responsible for _____."

3. Create a plan for how you will minimize the chance that your red flags and vulnerabilities will negatively impact your recovery. This may involve regular implementation of ERP or focusing on self-compassion. Examples:

   "I tend to feel disgusted around public trash cans and prefer avoiding being near them. I will touch public trash cans at least twice each time I leave my home."

   "My intrusive thoughts about harming someone can easily throw me off. I will create a card-matching game of harm thoughts that I can play each day, and I'll keep a sticky note with a harm thought where I will see it daily."

We humans are very good at finding excuses to not practice healthy behaviors. This can easily sabotage your progress and contribute to having a setback. Examples of excuses include:

- I feel so good right now. I don't want to ruin my day by doing ERP.

- I can do this ritual just this once. One time won't hurt.

- I'm too stressed out at work right now.

- I'm too tired to do ERP.

Also, notice how you can justify avoiding discomfort with "buts." Let's look at some typical examples:

- I could benefit from doing ERP today, *but* I'm too tired.

- My RP plan is to only wash for thirty seconds after using the bathroom, *but* I have an important presentation at work, and I'll be uncomfortable if I stick with my plan.

"But" is a common word used to discount what preceded it. Get off your "buts" by replacing the "but" with "and." Notice whether that seems more flexible to you.

Exercise: Excuses, Excuses

Make a list of ways you justify giving in to your OCD. After reviewing your list, do you see any "buts"? If so, rewrite it with the word "and" instead of "but." Next, what is a good response to these excuses? For example: a response to "I could benefit from doing ERP today, but I'm too tired" might be "Excellent. Doing ERP when I'm tired might provide me with a great learning experience."

Your relationship with your OCD symptoms changes as your symptoms become more manageable. As you find yourself with more time because you are spending less time on rituals, you may find that you have new anxiety. This may have to do with all the choices you have for how to spend your time. You may not have ever felt you had choices in how to live your life. You may find yourself with less anxiety—and this is anxiety provoking! It isn't uncommon for people to think *When is the other shoe going to drop?*

You may feel a full range of emotions about things you missed as a result of having OCD. It is normal to be touched by feelings of loss. Grieving is a natural reaction to loss and involves a full range of emotions. You may feel the loss of the false comfort that your compulsions gave you, even though it was temporary. On one hand you may miss that; on the other, you may feel angry or sad about the costs of your compulsions. Emotions associated with grieving can be complex and confusing at times. Allow yourself to grieve the losses you have experienced as a result of your OCD. As a way of honoring your feelings, you may have new activities that you want to do. If you're grieving the time you lost with family and friends, you may want to schedule activities with these loved ones. This can feel meaningful and special.

You can also replace the time you once spent doing compulsions with time doing meaningful activities. This can be fun, exciting, and fulfilling. Is there a skill you have always wanted to learn? Have you always wanted to get involved in your community? Do you want to make new friends? Make a list. Even if several things that you want to do may induce anxiety, include these on your list. Just as you slowly developed your ERP practice, you can start slowly with integrating new activities into your day.

Live Your Life with PASSION

Regardless of how beaten down by your OCD you may feel from time to time, you can live your life with passion.

P—Pause, Pivot, and Proceed toward what is important to you.

A—Accept your internal and external experiences as they show up.

S—Strengthen your stance: Stand tall, sternum lifted, shoulders back, and Step in the direction you want to go in.

S—Self-compassion practice and Self-care are fundamental.

I—Invite opportunities to practice exposure and open up to new experiences with curiosity, regardless of your discomfort.

O—Observe your thoughts, feelings, and sensations.

N—Now, stay present and aware of mental time travel to the past and future.

Visit http://www.newharbinger.com/51024 for a handout of this acronym that you can print out and post somewhere you can easily see it.

As you work on living with P-A-S-S-I-O-N, you can more easily make flexible decisions that lead to a life of vitality. You can make choices that are independent from your OCD. And you'll feel stronger and more satisfied in life.

Acknowledgments

A number of colleagues have contributed to my development of the ideas, skills, and information in this book. My professional communities from International OCD Foundation, Association for Contextual and Behavioral Sciences, Anxiety and Depression Association of America, and Association for Behavioral and Cognitive Therapies have provided excellent trainings and conferences that have shaped the ideas in this book. Special thanks to leaders in the field of OCD treatment who were particularly influential: C. Alec Pollard, the three Jons (Jonathan Abramowitz, Jonathan Grayson, and Jon Hershfield), Edna Foa, Reid Wilson, and Sally Winston. Thank you, Michelle Craske, for your research on inhibitory learning.

Thank you to Jeff Szymanski for introducing me to ACT and providing trainings in how to integrate ACT with people who have OCD. It's been a game changer. Steven Hayes, Lisa Coyne, Mike Twohig, Kelly Wilson, Robyn Walser, John Forsyth, Patricia Zurita-Ona, Russ Harris, and Louise Hayes are particularly influential.

Thank you, Jon Hart, for presenting on the importance of self-compassion at conferences long before it was popular. Thanks to leaders in self compassion practices who have taught me so much: Paul Gilbert, Chris Germer, Kristin Neff, and Stan Steindl.

I am grateful for the wisdom of Thich Nhat Hanh, Tara Brach, Jack Kornfield, Pema Chodron, and Fabrizio Didonna in their work on mindfulness practices.

This book would not be possible without the wonderful editorial staff at New Harbinger Publications. Thank you to Jess O'Brien, Vicraj Gill, and Kristi Hein for your expert and brilliant guidance. This book was written during the COVID-19 pandemic, and I contracted COVID-19 close to my manuscript deadline. Vicraj Gill went above and beyond to provide extra editorial support to me while I was recovering.

Thank you, Mark Sisti, PhD, ACT trainer and a Shodan in aikido, for generously sharing your time and wisdom with me as we had a wonderful conversation about the principles of aikido.

Special thanks to my friend and colleague Eric Goodman, PhD, who generously provided feedback on the manuscript. Over the last couple of decades, we have we have independently pursued similar ideas, collaborated, and followed a similar path professionally.

Thank you, Robert Leahy, for your wonderful presentation at ADAA in 2008, "Approaches to Treatment-Resistant Anxiety," that has been a source of inspiration for my work.

Prior to writing this book, a community of writers who are therapists, Psychwriters, led by Chris Willard and Michael Alcee, provided valuable feedback and encouragement. Paula Smith, Stefanie Haug, Jennifer Murphy, Caroline Hexdall, Emily Lapolice, Debbie Heiser, and Judy Silvan, I am grateful for your helpful comments. Thank you, Debbie Heiser, for inviting me to participate in Stump the Editor meetings with Hara Estroff Marano. Thank you, Hara Estroff Marano, for the helpful feedback on my initial ideas for this book. Thanks to writing coach Melissa Kirk for helping me believe that I'm capable of writing a book.

I want to thank my husband, Steve, for his loving support and encouragement. Many thanks to my family for all the love, support, and encouragement: Mom, Pam, Peggy, Tresa, and Lindsey. Thank you to my friend and colleague Cynthia Hutchins, for your wise feedback and encouragement over the span of our careers.

My journey into specialization in anxiety disorders and OCD would not be possible without the mentorship of Jim Wilson. I am grateful for all the education and support you have provided me.

I would like to extend my gratitude to all the clients who have taught me so much about what it's like to have OCD. I am grateful for the wealth of information you have taught me.

Thank you for reading this book. May you flexibly engage in a life that's meaningful to you and live free of the OCD rules.

References

Abramowitz, Jonathan S. 2018. *Getting Over OCD: A 10-Step Workbook for Taking Back Your Life.* 2nd ed. New York: Guilford Press.

Abramowitz, Jonathan S., Donald H. Baucom, Michael G. Wheaton, Sara Boeding, Laura E. Fabricant, Christine Paprocki, and Melanie S. Fischer. 2013. "Enhancing Exposure and Response Prevention for OCD: A Couple-Based Approach." *Behavior Modification* 37(2): 189–210.

Abramowitz, Jonathan S., Brett J. Deacon, and Stephen P. H. Whiteside. 2019. *Exposure Therapy for Anxiety: Principles and Practice.* 2nd ed. New York: Guilford Press.

Baer, Lee. 2001. *The Imp of the Mind: Exploring the Silent Epidemic of Obsessive Bad Thoughts.* New York: Dutton.

Bouchard, Catherine, Josée Rhéaume, and Robert Ladouceur. 1999. "Responsibility and Perfectionism in OCD: An Experimental Study." *Behavioral Research and Therapy* 37(3): 239–248.

Brewer, Judson. 2021. *Unwinding Anxiety: New Science Shows How to Break the Cycles of Worry and Fear to Heal Your Mind.* New York: Avery.

Clark, David A. 2020. *Cognitive-Behavioral Therapy for OCD and Its Subtypes.* 2nd ed. New York: Guilford Press.

Craske, Michelle G., Katherina Kircanski, Moriel Zelikowsky, Jayson Mystkowski, Najwa Chowdhury, and Aaron Baker. 2008. "Optimizing Inhibitory Learning During Exposure Therapy." *Behavioral Research and Therapy* 46(1): 5–27.

Craske, Michelle G., Michael Treanor, Christopher C. Conway, and Tomislav Zbozinek. 2014. "Maximizing Exposure Therapy: An Inhibitory Learning Approach." *Behavior Research and Therapy* 58: 10–23.

Didonna, Fabrizio. 2009. "Mindfulness and Obsessive-Compulsive Disorder: Developing a Way to Trust and Validate One's Internal Experience." In *Clinical Handbook of Mindfulness*, edited by Fabrizio Didonna, 189–220. New York: Springer.

Didonna, Fabrizio. 2020. *Mindfulness-Based Cognitive Therapy for OCD*. New York: Guilford Press.

Didonna, Fabrizio, Roberta Rossi, Clarissa Ferrari, Luca Iani, Laura Pedrini, Nicoletta Rossi, Erica Xodo, and Mariangela Lanfredi. 2019. "Relations of Mindfulness Facets and Psychological Symptoms Among Individuals with a Diagnosis of Obsessive-Compulsive Disorder, Major Depressive Disorder, or Borderline Personality Disorder." *Psychology and Psychotherapy: Theory, Research and Practice* 92(1): 112–130.

Flett, Gordon L., and Paul L. Hewitt. 2002. "Perfectionism and Maladjustment: An Overview of Theoretical, Definitional, and Treatment Issues." In *Perfectionism: Theory, Research and Treatment*, edited by Gordon L. Flett and Paul L. Hewitt, 5–31. Washington, DC: American Psychological Association.

Foa, Edna, and Michael J. Kozak. 1986. "Emotional Processing of Fear: Exposure to Corrective Information." *Psychological Bulletin* 99(1): 20–35.

Frost, Randy O., and Patricia M. DiBartolo. 2002. "Perfectionism, Anxiety and Obsessive-Compulsive Disorder." In *Perfectionism Theory, Research, and Treatment*, edited by Gordon L. Flett and Paul L. Hewitt, 341–371. Washington, DC: American Psychological Association.

Frost, Randy O., Richard Heimberg, Craig Holt, Jill Mattia, and Amy Neubauer. 1993. "A Comparison of Two Measures of Perfectionism." *Personality and Individual Differences* 14: 119–126.

Germer, Christopher, and Kristin Neff. 2019. *Teaching the Mindful Self-Compassion Program: A Guide for Professionals*. New York: Guilford Press.

Gilbert, Paul. 2009. *The Compassionate Mind*. London: Constable.

Gilbert, Paul. 2022. "Introducing and Developing CFT Functions and Competencies." In *Compassion Focused Therapy*, edited by Paul Gilbert and Gregoris Simos, 243–272. New York: Routledge.

Gilbert, Paul, and Dennis Tirch. 2009. "Emotional Memory, Mindfulness and Compassion." In *Clinical Handbook of Mindfulness*, edited by Fabrizio Didonna, 99–110. New York: Springer.

Grayson, Jonathan. 2014. *Freedom from Obsessive-Compulsive Disorder: A Personalized Recovery Program for Living with Uncertainty*. Updated ed. New York: Penguin Group.

Harris, Russ. 2009. *ACT Made Simple: An Easy-To-Read Primer on Acceptance and Commitment Therapy.* Oakland, CA: New Harbinger Publications.

Hayes, Steven C., Kirk D. Strosahl, and Kelly G. Wilson. 2012. *Acceptance and Commitment Therapy: The Process and Practice of Mindful Change.* 2nd ed. New York: Guilford Press.

Hershfield, Jon, and Tom Corboy. 2020. *The Mindfulness Workbook for OCD: A Guide to Overcoming Obsessions and Compulsions Using Mindfulness and Cognitive Behavioral Therapy.* 2nd ed. Oakland, CA: New Harbinger Publications.

Hershfield, Jon, and Shala Nicely. 2017. *Everyday Mindfulness for OCD: Tips, Tricks, and Skills for Living Joyfully.* Oakland, CA: New Harbinger Publications.

Kämpf, Maike S., Philipp Kanske, Alexandra Kleiman, Anke Haberkamp, Julia Glombiewski, and Cornelia Exner. 2022. "Empathy, Compassion and Theory of Mind in Obsessive-Compulsive Disorder." *Psychology and Psychotherapy: Theory, Research and Practice* 95: 1–17.

Kashdan, Todd. 2009. *Curious?: Discover the Missing Ingredient to a Fulfilling Life.* New York: HarperCollins e-books.

Kemp, Jennifer. 2020. *Understanding Perfectionism.* e-book.

MacBeth, Angus, and Andrew Gumley. 2012. "Compassion: A Meta-Analysis of the Association Between Self-Compassion and Psychopathology." *Clinical Psychology Review* 32(6): 545–552.

McGrath, Patrick. 2006. *Don't Try Harder, Try Different: A Workbook for Managing Anxiety and Stress.*

Neff, Kristin. 2011. *Self-Compassion: The Proven Power of Being Kind to Yourself.* New York: William Morrow.

Neff, Kristin, Phoebe Long, Marissa Knox, Oliver Davidson, Ashley Kuchar, Andrew Costigan, Zachary Willamson, Nicolaş Rohleder, Istvan Toth-Kiraly, and Juliana G. Breines. 2018. "The Forest and the Trees: Examining the Association of Self-Compassion and Its Positive and Negative Components with Psychological Functioning." *Self and Identity* 17(6): 627–645.

Obsessive Compulsive Cognitions Working Group. 1997. "Cognitive Assessment of Obsessive-Compulsive Disorder." *Behavior Research and Therapy* 35(7): 667–681.

Pollard, Alec C. 2004. "How I Treat Scrupulosity and Religious Obsessions." *OCD Newsletter* 18(4, Summer).

Quinlan, Kimberley. 2021. *The Self-Compassion Workbook for OCD: Lean into Your Fear, Manage Difficult Emotions, and Focus On Recovery.* Oakland, CA: New Harbinger Publications.

Rachman, Stanley J., and Padmal de Silva. 1978. "Abnormal and Normal Obsessions." *Behavior Research and Therapy* 16(4): 233–248.

Radomsky, Adam S., Michel J. Dugas, Gillian M. Alcolado, and Stefanie L. Lavoie. 2014. "When More Is Less: Doubt, Repetition, Memory, Metamemory, and Compulsive Checking in OCD." *Behavior Research and Therapy* 59(August): 30–39.

Sharma, Eesha, Lavanya P. Sharma, Srinivas Balachander, Boyee Lin, Harshini Manohar, Puneet Khanna, et al. 2021. "Comorbidities in Obsessive-Compulsive Disorder Across the Lifespan: A Systematic Review and Meta-Analysis." *Frontiers in Psychiatry* 12(November): Article 703701.

Szentágotai-Tatar, Aurora, Diana-Mirela Nechita, and Andrei C. Miu. 2020. "Shame in Anxiety and Obsessive-Compulsive Disorders." *Current Psychiatry Reports* 22(16).

Taylor, Steven. 2002. "Cognition in Obsessive Compulsive Disorder: An Overview." In *Cognitive Approaches to Obsessions and Compulsions: Theory, Assessment, and Treatment,* edited by Randy O. Frost and Gayle Steketee, 1–12. Amsterdam: Elsevier Science.

Wegner, Daniel. 1994. *White Bears and Other Unwanted Thoughts: Suppression, Obsession, and the Psychology of Mental Control.* New York: Guilford Press.

Weingarden, Hilary, and Keith D. Renshaw. 2015. "Shame in the Obsessive Compulsive Related Disorders: A Conceptual Review." *Journal of Affective Disorders* 171(January): 74–84.

Wilson, Reid. 2016. *Stopping the Noise in Your Head: The New Way to Overcome Anxiety and Worry.* Deerfield Beach, FL: Health Communications.

Kim Rockwell-Evans, PhD, is a licensed professional counselor and licensed marriage and family therapist with more than thirty-five years of experience treating children, adolescents, and adults. She is in private practice at OCD and Anxiety Specialists of Dallas in Richardson, TX; where she specializes in treating obsessive-compulsive disorder (OCD) and anxiety disorders.

Real change *is* possible

For more than forty-five years, New Harbinger has published proven-effective self-help books and pioneering workbooks to help readers of all ages and backgrounds improve mental health and well-being, and achieve lasting personal growth. In addition, our spirituality books offer profound guidance for deepening awareness and cultivating healing, self-discovery, and fulfillment.

Founded by psychologist Matthew McKay and Patrick Fanning, New Harbinger is proud to be an independent, employee-owned company. Our books reflect our core values of integrity, innovation, commitment, sustainability, compassion, and trust. Written by leaders in the field and recommended by therapists worldwide, New Harbinger books are practical, accessible, and provide real tools for real change.

newharbingerpublications

MORE BOOKS from
NEW HARBINGER PUBLICATIONS

Did you know there are **free tools** you can download for this book?

Free tools are things like **worksheets, guided meditation exercises,** and **more** that will help you get the most out of your book.

You can download free tools for this book—whether you bought or borrowed it, in any format, from any source—from the New Harbinger website. All you need is a NewHarbinger.com account. Just use the URL provided in this book to view the free tools that are available for it. Then, click on the "download" button for the free tool you want, and follow the prompts that appear to log in to your NewHarbinger.com account and download the material.

You can also save the free tools for this book to your **Free Tools Library** so you can access them again anytime, just by logging in to your account! Just look for this button on the book's free tools page.

+ Save this to my free tools library

If you need help accessing or downloading free tools, visit **newharbinger.com/faq** or contact us at **customerservice@newharbinger.com**.